Oct. 12, 1981

Dear Kathie;

To a Special and
Most beautiful
Puppet!
a great friend too!

Luv from
Nancy, "Ben F." and
staff

PUPPETRY
and the
ART OF STORY CREATION

By Nancy Renfro

Published by Nancy Renfro Studios
Puppetry in Education Series

A PUPPET CORNER IN EVERY LIBRARY

PUPPETRY AND THE ART OF STORY CREATION

PUPPETRY AND CREATIVE DRAMATICS IN STORYTELLING

Published in the United States of America by
Nancy Renfro Studios 1117 W. 9th Street, Austin, Texas 78703
ISBN # 0-931044-02-2
All photographs and illustrations by Nancy Renfro, unless otherwise noted

COVER CREDITS
front: Abstract puppets by Michelle Pelletier and Ketti Davison, Clearspring Elementary School, under the direction of Geraldine Pressley
back: Body puppet by James Petrosky, Texas State School for the Deaf, under the direction of Cynthia Roup

To be one's own rainmaker

Helen Hayes

ACKNOWLEDGEMENTS

My thanks to the following, without whom this book would not be what it is:

The East Campus, Texas State School for the Deaf—to its administration, staff and children for the opportunity to develop new ideas in puppetry for the deaf. I feel fortunate to have worked with librarian Marion Granberry and rhythm teacher Cynthia Roup, both of whom have allowed joyous things to happen. I thank, also, Jim Howze and Sue Drake for their administrative support.

Robert T. Renfro, my husband—for his undying faith in my work.

Ann Weiss Schwalb, children's librarian, Tredyffrin Public Library of Strafford, Pennsylvania—to an invaluable friend, chief editor and consultant for being instrumental in initiating this series of books.

Margaret Roberts of Austin, Texas—for serving as assistant editor.

Kirby Hall, College Preparatory School of Austin, and drama instructor, Brendan Kenny—for participating in projects incorporated into this book.

Clearspring Elementary School of San Antonio and staff Ester Pape and Geraldine Pressley—for joining me in these projects.

Judy Schwab of the Englishtown School District of New Jersey—to a perceptive and talented teacher of art.

Connie Champlin, Media Specialist of Omaha, Nebraska—for her assistance and support.

Texas and Georgia State teachers and librarians—for their inspiring puppet designs during workshop participation.

Puppeteers of America and The Puppetry in Education organizations—for their support and influence on my work, and their dedication to the betterment of puppetry.

TABLE OF CONTENTS

BODY PUPPET—Candy Gert

INTRODUCTION

Most of us are observers of other people's stories. We sometimes live out these stories, these personal histories and legends, created by authors both known and unknown. But while the world's stories evolve, we do not think of ourselves as creators of stories. Our mysterious inner worlds remain guarded secrets, lost to the world and to ourselves. Once we realize, however, how natural is the process of story creation, we, too, can add to that panoply of ideas.

I was brought up to believe that ALL stories are found in books. I did not yet know that I am a story and you are a story and that within us are infinite other stories. To sequence and dramatize events, to make them occur, at least for the moment, larger than life, suspended in time and space, is a capacity uniquely characteristic to all of us. I did not attempt my first story until I was twenty-six years old and became involved with puppetry. I found that I needed a story, not one of the classic folk tales, but a contemporary story, uniquely suited to the children with whom I was working. With copyright laws so complex, I did not want to take the chance of infringing upon another author's work. The only solution was to write one myself.

Conceptualizing an original story had never occurred to me. As I began this new undertaking, I was surrounded by a sea of vagueness, confusion and vacuity. How does one begin a story? An outline, I knew, was the proper way to begin, but alas, I had never been very comfortable (nor, for that matter, very competent with) writing outlines. A new wrinkle was desperately needed.

I found that anywhere one begins writing a story becomes, in fact, the beginning. The important thing then, is *to begin*. In my case, I closed my eyes and began by conceiving of a title—it then became the seed of an idea and a fitting start from which other ideas could germinate. Much as a painting grows on the canvas, the initial seed of an idea grew into an entire story.

Because I was not limited by any outline, my story branched out in any direction I chose; the story began to evolve, with diverse elements fitting together like pieces of a puzzle. But unlike a puzzle, the pieces of my story—the ideas—were not rigid; instead they were malleable, allowing my imagination rather than the outline to lead the way. If I came to a dead end, I simply backed up a bit and tried a different course. The alternatives were both productive and enjoyable, enabling me to explore many possibilities before arriving at a result that finally satisfied me.

Given freedom, children are marvelous creators of stories. Their natural, intuitive gifts in almost all the arts, however, are structured too much and too early in an educational system sometimes too concerned with logic. As children grow older and are repeatedly subjected to this structuring process, the flow of ideas, and the very essence of creativity often becomes dormant and sometimes diminishes entirely. It is my hope that this book will help counteract some of the restrictions by demonstrating simple techniques of creating stories for puppet productions.

Now, let's begin!

CREATING A STORY

The Beginning

There are as many beginnings to a puppet play as there are people. Although each of us might feel more comfortable starting from a different vantage point, nevertheless we must all begin somewhere. But where? First, start with an idea, one about which you are enthusiastic or in which you strongly believe. If you are not fond of this idea in the initial stage, then the struggle between joy and frustration that you will experience in developing this idea could easily lead to an unsatisfying solution. Therefore the essence of a good beginning is a strong friendship with a good idea, an idea that is important to you.

Where can ideas be found? In many places, for each of us carries around a bottomless sack of them. Ideas may be found in a:

TITLE SENTENCE

A title sentence, made up or taken from another source, is a good lead for a story. Have the students help make up a list to have on hand, such as: *How the Giraffe Got its Long Neck*; *A Funny Thing Happened on the Way to McDonald's*; *I've Got a Super Secret*; *The Day the World Went Crazy*; *The Gift*; *An Incredible New Discovery*; *The Award I Won*; *How I Spent a Million Dollars.*

PERSON

A fictitious or real person, such as a relative, friend, or historic figure, may inspire a story. For example: *an eccentric movie star*; *a temperamental sports player*; *an unknown creature from outer space*; *a rich aunt*; *Thomas Edison*; *Picasso*; *the school's principal.*

EXPERIENCE

Personal experiences are easy to conjure up and create a colorful background for a story. Have the group tell about experiences, such as having: *a broken bone*; *burnt cookies*; *a toothache*; *a vacation*; *a fight.*

MESSAGE

An idea or cause about which someone feels strongly and wishes to tell the world is a good basis for making up a story. Discuss with the students their pet peeves, protests, statements concerning such things as bad manners, a new building in town, the latest fashion or car design, politics, or pollution. Resulting examples might be: *people who are too noisy while eating soup; children's lib*; *purple sneakers*; *don't litter*; *gentlemen before ladies or ladies before gentlemen?*

WORD

Words can spark an unusual story idea. Have the children search out special words in the dictionary, which may also enhance language skills. Short skits based on selected words can help develop vocabulary, as well as writing skills. Some examples are: *soporific*; *pompous*; *justice*; *extraneous*; *grotesque*; *magnificent.* Imaginary words may also be fun to explore, à la Dr. Seuss, like: *Ittymitty Matamoris*; *the Giant Grouchooshoot*; *the Funny Weedle.*

LOOK INTO THE FUTURE

Predictions of the future play upon the student's penchant for science fiction. Discuss with them what the future might be like. A story could incorporate such themes as: *a funny uncle*; *a unique house*; *an incredible factory*; *a strange animal*; *an unusual sports game.*

POEM OR RIDDLE

An original or found poem or riddle makes an excellent story plot. Check *Poetry Index* to find poems on various subjects or browse through any collection of poetry to find a poem that appeals to you. Poetry written by students themselves, such as *The Me Nobody Knows*, might make a penetrating basis for a story.

JOURNEY

A real or imaginary journey could easily take one on an adventure to the unknown. Have the students discuss their own journeys, both real and imagined as well as some they wish to take. For example: *a trip to the big city*; *a journey through "Terrible-Land"*; *an underwater voyage*; *a journey into the past*; *an imaginary route to school*; *a trip to an unknown planet.*

A FUNNY WEEDLE

A UNIQUE HOUSE

EXTRANEOUS

NEWSPAPER CLIPPING

Newspapers abound with ideas for stories. Have the student skim the newspaper and cut out articles, headlines, and pictures of special interest to put on the bulletin board for discussion. Stories can be inspired by clippings such as: *an exciting football game*; *a socialite's party*; *animal pictures*; *a funny cartoon*; *a political election.*

SETTING

A setting, whether imaginary or real, could serve as a backdrop for a story. Have the children describe in detail a particular setting of interest, such as: *a school*; *a spaceship*; *their room*; *an ocean liner*; *an upside-down, inside-out land.* Use this descriptive setting to develop a story.

OBJECT OR THING

Objects and things make excellent sources of inspiration and can trigger a vast array of ideas from which to work. Have the students bring in a collection of random objects to display for discussion, such as: *a pencil*; *a toy telephone*; *a rope*; *a balloon*; *a bone*; *a teapot*; *a rose.* Inaccessible or imaginary objects may also be considered, such as: *a walking chair*; *a road*; *a haunted house*; *a magic box*; *an object from outer space.*

A STORY AROUND AN OBJECT/EGG—Michelle Pelletier and Ketti Davison **Abstract puppet**

A STORY AROUND AN OBJECT/TRASH CAN
Alley Cat and Trash Can—Michael Daily and Carey Kriger

A STORY AROUND A WORK OF ART—Rousseau's "The Sleeping Gypsy"
Cardboard Bunraku Puppet by Nancy Renfro, operated by Laura Lyon

WORK OF ART

Almost any work of art—music, painting, or sculpture by established artists or by the students themselves—create marvelous images from which to extract ideas. Collaborate with the music or art teacher and study works of art with the students. Ask them to make up a story from some of the examples, such as: Miro's painting *The Harlequin's Carnival;* Rousseau's *The Sleeping Gypsy;* Rodin's sculpture *The Thinker;* Beethoven's musical score *5th Symphony.*

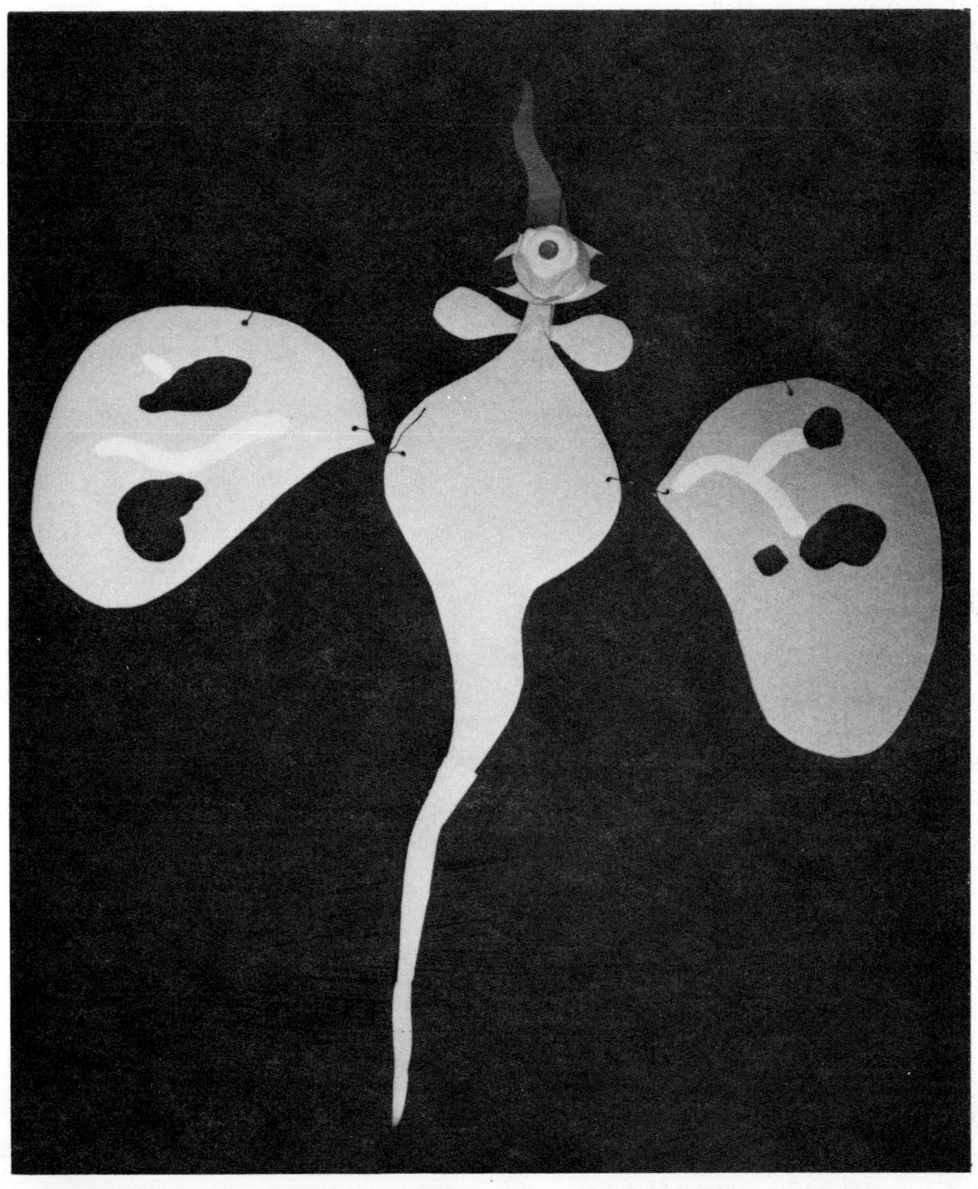

A STORY AROUND A WORK OF ART—Miro's "The Harlequin's Carnival" Cardboard String Puppet

A STORY FROM A PAINTING—Mondrian's Broadway Boogie-Woogie
Animated Cardboard Puppet

The Opening

The first few minutes of any puppet play are the most critical, for they should set the tone of the story as well as the "snare" that captivates the audience. Therefore, special attention should be given to the first impressions the audience receives as the curtain rises. Will the entertainment begin with an air of suspense or with a festive carnival mood, with a raucous argument or with silence? Will a song be sung or a terrifying soliloquy be blasted?

Whether drama or comedy, a play can open with a bang or more quietly. It is, perhaps, most difficult to begin with a bang, such as a noisy argument, for once struck, the remainder of the story can easily become anti-climactic. Building up gradually from a lower to a higher level of action is an easier approach for the novice. The important consideration to keep in mind is that a good story, like a good magic performance, should not spring *all* the surprises at the beginning. For example, if all the cast, scenery, and props appear within the first few minutes of the story, there will be nothing new with which to surprise the audience as the story unravels.

Remember to scatter these elements throughout the story; bring out your surprises one by one to build up the audience's anticipation!

Preparing The Audience

What kind of mood will your audience be in immediately prior to the story or show? A restless or excited audience needs to be coaxed into an appropriate mood before the show. Following are some suggestions to help establish the proper mood:

Use music. Music, one of the world's best mood setters, may be played before the show begins. Live music is particularly enjoyable, but records or prerecorded music are also fine. Be sure to select pieces appropriate to the particular character of the show, such as *Star Wars* for science fiction, *Carnival of the Animals* for animal stories, or Christmas melodies for Christmas tales. There is an infinite selection of records and cassettes from which to choose. For example, piano-roll, calliope, flute, moog-synthesizer, ragtime, harp, and country-western are but a few of the diverse choices with which to tantalize the audience.

Talk to your audience. A teacher, librarian, or other adult who works with children may appear to warm up the audience before the play begins. Asking the audience questions about things pertaining to the show (with or without puppets) helps establish a familiarity with the subject matter of the play, as well as a sense of anticipation. For instance, a story with an opossum character could start with a discussion of the special characteristics of an opossum. The commentator could ask about the unique traits of this animal, eliciting the information that it is a marsupial with a pouch, and that it gives birth to thirteen babies tiny enough to fit into a teaspoon, etc. A show that takes place in a foreign country could open with a discussion about that place. Another good source of conversation is to allow the children to share their own experiences with puppets and shows.

Create a setting for the audience. The room, itself, could help set the mood of the show. A Halloween event could be held in a room with dimmed lights and a lighted jack-o-lantern; a circus theme could be enhanced by circus posters and colorful balloons. For science fiction, glowing planets and stars on the walls could be created by using blacklights and phosphorescent paint; fish mobiles (made by some of the classes) could be hung for an underwater theme.

Opening The Production

Now that you have set the stage by using music, talking to the audience, or creating an appropriate setting for the viewers, the next thing to consider is how you will signal the commencement of the story itself. There are various ways. For example:

An emcee may announce or lead into the story, unseen, from behind the stage. One of the most exciting openings I have ever witnessed was in a New York production called *The Globerlinks are Coming!* Drama and suspense increased as the lights suddenly dimmed. Then a desperate, agitated voice penetrated the darkness with a news release that mysterious creatures had been sighted after landing on earth. Handled in Orson Welles' *War of the Worlds* fashion, this opening was so real that it almost frightened the audience. It was a 'bang' of a beginning, but one skillfully sustained throughout the production.

A story, of course, may be just as successful begun with a whispering voice or a straightforward, everyday voice, depending upon the desired effect. The traditional "Once upon a time . . ." remains an effective way to begin any story, for it automatically draws the audience into a good story listening mood. Audiences never tire of following these magical words into the land of make-believe.

An emcee may announce the story from frontstage. The emcee or moderator may simply stand in front of the stage and recite a carefully thought out introduction. A sequence might be as follows: First recite a poem or riddle that sets the tone of the story; then announce the story and tell the audience something special about the story, such as how it evolved, where it came from, etc. Or perhaps show the audience an object (such as a small cradle, a dog bone, or a bunch of keys) around which the story revolves; then ask questions or speak wise words to initiate a discussion about it with the audience.

A narrator may narrate the story frontstage or backstage and remain there during the entire show. This person may narrate the entire story, which is then essentially pantomimed, or may participate only occasionally to interrupt the story in a "Kukla, Fran and Ollie" approach, making comments, asking questions and acting as a go-between for the audience and the story. This method of strong leadership insures greater intimacy as well as control of the audience; it works particularly well with young children. The narrator may consider dressing in a costume. For example, Nancy Staub's Puppet Playhouse of New Orleans presented a delightful version of *The Rabbit with Red Wings,* narrated by Luis Burroso in a hillbilly outfit, complete with patched overalls, straw hat, and a scraggly long black beard! A tremendously warm personality, he spoke with the twangy accent of the hills of the South and held a book on his lap. As he read from it, he knew just when to draw out certain words, when to make eye contact with the audience, and when to jump up in excitement to talk with the rabbit about something. The narrator can be as colorful as the show itself; the role of narrator is particularly suited to the teenager or older child who is interested in developing acting skills. Other ideas to try are a strange creature in science fiction, or Mother Goose in a presentation of nursery rhymes.

A puppet narrator or emcee may announce the story. This character may be part of the official cast or may be a totally unrelated character, perhaps one that has become a regular friend of the children's. It may be a familiar animal friend, an eccentric author, or a visitor from another country or galaxy. A story with a special theme might incorporate a puppet narrator to pull the work together: a lifeguard in a beach tale, a talking tree in a forest story, or even a symbol such as a narrator—teardrop in a tale of woe and misery.

A story may simply begin without any formal introduction. A story could open in the middle of a dramatic argument, abruptly stop, and finally be followed by dialogue which explains the problem. Or perhaps a man is quietly planting a seed to music; nothing much seems to be happening, when suddenly the seed begins to grow and grow—right into a most absurd walking creature, one that causes all sorts of problems as the story unfolds.

With this type of beginning, be sure that the audience understands that the show is ready to start. The pre-show mood music should be turned off and total silence should reign. Dim the lights. Let silence prevail for a few seconds, then begin.

No matter how you choose to handle the narration of your production be careful *Not* to begin any show with a long announcement about its creators, the performers, or bibliographic information. Such material is often dull, technical and certainly alien to the mood of the entertainment. If it is desired that the storytellers be formally introduced at the beginning, make it short and simple. "We have the pleasure to present to you today . . ." will suffice. On the other hand, after the performance the creators or performers may be introduced in detail to the audience, questions asked, and discussion initiated. Children, particularly older ones, are interested in the mechanics of any show and would enjoy a visit backstage, if the puppeteers consent.

The audience is now in the proper frame of mind to enjoy your presentation. Remember that the opening scene is essentially a concentrated impression of what is to come. Because this initial visual impact is vitally important, the opening should be carefully designed as to 1) *characters*; 2) *action*; and 3) *setting*. Here are some questions to help you capture the audience with the opening scene:

CHARACTERS

What characters will open up the story? It is most difficult to stage a quality show that begins with all the cast entering at once. Though I should not like to rule the idea out, tread carefully when using this approach. Presenting the entire cast too soon, at best, dulls the audience's anticipation of good things to come and, at worst, can make your production confusing and difficult to follow. Therefore, unless you want to achieve a particular effect or have a legitimate reason for opening with many characters, do not use this method; think instead in terms of gradually introducing your cast one or two players at a time as the story unfolds.

ACTION

What action will open up the story? The action opening a story may be ap-

Luis Burroso in "The Rabbit with Red Wings", by the Puppet Playhouse

proached in a low-keyed way or with a bang.

A low-keyed approach, a simple action that is built upon gradually, is a safe beginning, one that more readily insures the audience's full attention. It is a technique highly regarded among professionals. For example: A single puppet might begin gradually pulling things out of a closet or box until the entire scene is cluttered; a puppet could be assembling a car or machine piece by piece encountering trouble in the process; or two puppets could be skipping rope to a song until the rope breaks; then introduce the conflict around which the story will revolve.

A "bang" approach begins with a great deal of action, such as two puppets frantically chasing each other or a noisy crowd gathering at a football game. Such an opening undoubtedly makes a greater initial impact upon the audience. It is here that the performers' finer skills are tested, in preventing a show that has opened on a high note from descending too low and possibly becoming anticlimactic.

SETTING

What will the stage setting be? A few simple props are sufficient to tell a good story. I have seen perhaps too many shows with elaborate backgrounds which made it difficult for the audience to see the puppets. Remember that the puppets must stand out to be seen. Scenic backgrounds are appropriate if the color schemes contrast with the puppets; good lighting will further help make the puppets stand out. Have someone view your rehearsal from the back of the room to check the visibility of the puppets.

Remember, too, to consider the mood of your story as you plan your settings. Color and light can be an effective part of beginning on a good note. For example, a ghost could be surrounded by a stage setting of eerie mist (low lights, squeezed puffs of "fog" from a plastic baby-powder bottle, and string cobwebs); a flower character could stand out against a rising sun washing a glow of warm colors on the background; or a science-fiction setting might open to eerie lighting and music with simple suggestions of a moonscape.

No matter how the story opens, let it be a beginning of which you are proud. In developing a story, it is important to believe in the beginning; it bolsters the spirit to put work and energy into the show. I rarely change my beginnings once they're designed, although the middle and endings undergo many revisions.

The Middle

Hatching and developing the plot are perhaps the most challenging aspects of story creation. In developing the plot, alternate ideas must be explored. Try different solutions! Do not be satisfied with the first idea that comes to mind, but instead try one idea, explore it, perhaps reject it, and try another. Have a brainstorming session with yourself. You will sometimes need to explore several possibilities in case one idea does not work; at other times you will need to combine several ideas into a single work. Remember that flexibility and an openness to ideas are the keys to creativity. If one thing does not work, try another. Above all, give the imagination freedom to travel at will; in so doing, creativity will surface.

Even the most imaginative stories, however, must be ordered in some way so that the audience can follow the action and enjoy the story. In particular, we can think of the following items as essential for developing any good story:

IDEA OR THEME
the unifying concept of the story.
EPISODES
the events of the story.
CONFLICTS
the "problems" that add tension and interest to the story.
CLIMAX
the resolution of the conflicts(s).

The Idea or Theme

A story is built around an idea or theme. Children's stories are often built around serious ideas. *Sleeping Beauty*, for example, dramatizes the theme of the regenerative power of love, as do all the frog-handsome prince stories. The old fashioned cautionary tales contain an actual statement of purpose at the end, and Aesop's fables also illustrate a specific moral.

Although it is not necessary to think in terms of a moral, you will find that stories naturally center around definite themes—hostility, friendship, love, and so on. A theme is important because it provides unity to a work. A clear sense of the idea or theme of a story can therefore help us decide what episodes to use, and in what order.

A consideration of theme, however, should never stand in the way of the first purpose of a puppet play, which is to provide lively entertainment. In a successful puppet play, just as in a successful fairy tale, it is clearly the story itself that captures the audience's attention. A story like *The Fisherman and His Wife,* for instance, does contain a significant moral about the consequences of greed and excessive pride, but it presents this theme with the accompaniment of magic, humor, conflict, and suspense.

The Episodes

Creating and expanding episodes

A story is composed of related events or episodes which move toward an ending. One of the most valuable skills a story-creator can learn is how to build a given situation into a well-rounded episode. A challenging exercise for students might be to expand random titles or "idea sentences" into complete episodes. Some examples follow:

Two cooks argue over the soup.
A man is lying on a hammock, reading a paper on a very, very hot day.
A small boy has gone to a scary movie by himself.
While walking down the street, a dog has found a bone.
A girl decides to swim in a rough ocean, although her parents have forbidden her to do so.
A baker will make his masterpiece creation.
An elephant is planning to eat his first meal of spaghetti.
An inexperienced painter has decided to paint a one hundred story building.
A fence separates two neighbors.
Someone has hiccups that will not stop.
Two people are competing for the star role in the circus.
Grandma's false teeth are creating problems.
Nobody wants to do the dishes.
A mouse avoids homework and gets into trouble.

In creating a story, allow plenty of time for the plot to unravel. Inexperienced writers often leave underdeveloped ideas which could be rounded out to create a fuller, more meaningful story. Although it is common to get an idea and incorporate it without further thought, it is worthwhile to remember that no idea is good enough; there is always room for improvement. I have often been excited initially about an idea which seemed excellent but upon further consideration, needed improvement or expansion. A one-minute sketch within a story, for example, may frequently be stretched into an event of three or even five minutes.

How does one stretch an idea? First, pinpoint an idea or event, then write it in the form of an idea sentence, and have a brainstorming session. What are all the words or images that come to mind with this idea? For example, begin with:

THE IDEA SENTENCE

Two cooks argue over the soup.

WORDS AND IMAGES

Pots and pans, *spoon*, stove, *taste*, aroma, *angry*, very angry, *battle*, *breaks plate over head*, minestrone, *fish*, *seafood gumbo*, dishwasher butts in, *boss is mad*, *customers are waiting*, *stir*, steaming soup, lots of steam, a fly, bubbling soup.

Now select words and images to be expanded upon and developed into an episode:

EXPANSION

One cook is sluggishly stirring a large pot of seafood gumbo. He hums a bit, utters some mumbo-jumbo, looks around to see whether anyone is looking, and steals a taste of soup (slurp). At that moment a silly fish pops its head up and squirts a stream of soup in the cook's face. (Use a water pistol) After wiping his face with a paper towel, the cook tries to catch the fish (splash splash) but can't. Soon the other cook appears, tastes the soup, makes a terrible face, and says it needs salt. The first cook consults with the fish; they both agree that the soup definitely does not need salt. Both cooks take turns tasting the soup. One keeps saying yes, the other no. The soup-tasting builds to a crescendo (more slurps), until the boss finally stumps in, yelling "Customers

are waiting! Where's the soup?" But by now the soup has disappeared. The cooks are so much in disagreement that they first begin hitting one another over the head with spoons, then breaking plates over one another's head, and finally they begin a full-fledged battle with pots and pans flying everywhere. (Use cardboard props with crashing sound effects backstage) The poor fish is caught in between. Both cooks are knocked unconscious and the fish plays nursemaid. The boss comes in, sees the hopeless mess, whisks the fish onto a plate and serves it to the impatient customers.

Developing a series of simple one-episode stories, such as the one above, is an easy way to begin teaching story-making skills to children. It requires from them both logic and concentration. These episodes may be linked together with a narrator and presented as a show of short skits. Once the students have created one- and two-episode stories, they may continue using and elaborating upon the principles suggested in the preceding pages to weave more complex stories.

Joining episodes into a story

No matter how well developed they are, episodes, alone, are not enough for a satisfying story. A series of events must be related in such a way as to build into a coherent whole. Thus in assembling a story we should ask ourselves:

What is the story about?
What are the episodes within the story?
How do these various episodes fit together?
How do they relate to a common end as well as to themselves?

Two key factors in fitting episodes into a story are *sequencing* and *flow*. Sequencing, an aspect with which many students have difficulty, is the stitching together of events into a consecutive, logical pattern. Flow is the smooth meshing together of events within the story. Together, they transform mere disjointed episodes into a unified whole.

To illustrate the difference, consider the following: "The king died. Later the queen died." Although these are episodes they are episodes with no clearly discernible relationship. An improvement would be: "Because the king died of poison, the queen died of grief." Now we have a kernal, however meager, of a story for now the events have an interrelationship to one another.

These linking skills may be strengthened through class exercise. After completing the exercises on expansion of idea sentences (see page 27), have the students use the same technique to arrange episodes in the proper order.

For example, one could ask: What episode might follow *two cooks argue over the soup* expanded episode? Here are some possibilities from a brainstorming session:

—The cooks wake in time to save the fish.
—The fish causes havoc with the customers.
—The fish jumps off the plate, and escapes out the door.

After the students have come up with several possibilities, have them choose a consecutive idea sentence they like and expand upon it. Now link the original and the newly developed episodes together. Suppose we choose the idea sentence above: *The fish causes havoc with the customers* to follow the original, expanded episode of *two cooks argue over the soup.* We left the original episode with the fish on a platter to be served to the customers by the Boss. We must ask:

—How does the fish create havoc?
—What are the limitations of its mobility?
—Who is the first customer it encounters?
—What role does the Boss play during this time?

Here are some suggestions for linking these two episodes:

—The Boss enters the dining room filled with impatient customers. He looks around carefully and spots a gentleman, who is rhythmically tapping his fork on the table. The gentleman looks on the verge of anger and is glaring at the Boss. The Boss decides to serve the fish to him.

—The Boss enters the dining room to find all the customers angry and impatient. They are all beckoning the Boss simultaneously to come to their tables. The Boss is utterly confused on which table to go to first. The fish, who can no longer bear the confusion decides to jump onto a grand lady's new wig, which start an outbreak of trouble in the dining room.

Conflicts

Conflicts are immensely important to a story, for they encompass both the events of the plot itself and the tension that lends it interest. A story which presents neither a problem nor a dissenting view, is more than likely an uninteresting one. Almost any good story contains some degree of conflict. Whether we are watching a frivolous comedy or absorbed in a serious drama, it is the conflict structuring the work that most powerfully draws our attention.

Teaching students the concept of "conflict"

"Conflict" is actually two or more forces in opposition in a story. One of the best ways to relay this concept to children is to help them understand the archetype good-versus-bad conflict, using examples such as a brave hero and an evil bandit, a wicked witch and a good little girl. The students will readily come up with examples of their own. Once they understand the basic good versus evil conflict, they can begin to understand more subtle conflicts, such as those which encompass feelings of sadness versus happiness, like versus dislike, etc.

Studying synonyms and antonyms could be the basis for discussing and developing some short exercises on conflicts. Have the students list pairs of opposites, such as:

love — hate
advantage — disadvantage
weak — strong
grotesque — beautiful
married — unmarried
soft — hard
selfish — unselfish

Have the students work in teams of two to create puppets or story situations utilizing these opposite words. For example, some puppets might be:

grotesque
a twisted tree
beautiful
a ravishing French poodle

soft
cotton
hard
steel

Some situations might easily be developed around these opposite words and eventually be incorporated into a story idea. For example, a conflict could evolve around a **twisted tree** and a ravishing **French poodle:**

—The French poodle could be terribly vain and constantly visits a clear pool beside the twisted tree to admire herself. The poodle persistently mocks the tree and compares herself to the tree's ugliness, until one day the tree saves the poodle's life by scaring away a vicious villain.

or a conflict for **cotton** and **steel:**

—An elephant has insomnia and decides to build a bed. He cannot decide what the best material is for bed-building and confers with his animal friends. One friend suggests cotton; another steel. The elephant experiments with both and discovers the advantages and disadvantages of these materials in the process. Which one makes the better elephant-bed?

Creating conflicts for a puppet play

How does the creator of a story or play find a conflict? The techniques are similar to those used in creating episodes, for the conflicts are naturally expressed through the events and the characters of the story.

An *object* as the focal point is often helpful. Mentioning or actually holding up a particular object before a brainstorming session can elicit innumerable ideas.

A ROPE, for example, could suggest a tug-of-war between two characters. The one who loses becomes miserable because he is a weakling. He searches for physical strength, only to find that it is not as important as he had estimated it to be.

Or a *ROPE* might refuse to stay knotted. All the characters try their most inventive knots on it, consult the highest authorities on knotting and finally search out the wisest Snake-Knot Wizard, who knows all the knots in the world.

A PAIR OF SCISSORS could be a destructive force, cutting up everything in its path. The characters must work together to end this destruction before it causes the end of the world. Or the scissors could be magic scissors, creating beautiful cut-out creatures for a sick child.

A GIANT DOG COLLAR could be far too big for all the dogs in the kingdom, inspiring a mad search around the countryside for a dog to fit the collar. A giant goofy looking dog is found at last. Upon being fit, the collar glows with magic and the giant dog begins to misuse his new powers; the rest of the cast then helps him find wisdom.

HAMBURGERS could inspire a scene in a famous fast-food restaurant, McDoodles or McDoggies (using dogs for a cast). Something has gone haywire with the hamburger-production line; the workers just cannot keep up with the customers. One of the cooks secretly invents a hamburger-making machine, which is a success but in turn causes new problems for the assembly line and the customers.

A RULER has been calibrated on an incorrect scale. As a result, an architect designs a city to the wrong scale, to the woe of its citizens who must cope with a life out of scale to everything. All sorts of problems ensue; life becomes chaotic. Perhaps the city is so big in scale that no one can climb the steps of city hall, eat at the tables, or reach the steering wheels of the cars.

The *central idea or title* is also a good starting point for developing a conflict.

HOW THE TURTLE GOT ITS CRACKS could inspire stories à la Rudyard Kipling. Could the turtle have been shattered in a bad fall and patched up again by all the animals? Could the turtle have been in a fight? Or could it have been tired of its original smoothly armored clothing and gone to one of the best designers in Paris for something with a little more pizazz?

I FOUND A MILLION DOLLARS might inspire many ideas through personal identification. Perhaps a character who loves ice cream, candy and cake spends it all on these things, then develops an incurable tummy-ache. She searches throughout the world for a cure. Or perhaps the character decides to give all the money away to five other characters, each of whom is very kind to the finder up until the moment of getting the money. Then all five of them greedily spend it, ignoring the central character, who learns that friendship cannot be bought. A sixth character, who did not receive any of the money, shows him true friendship, by befriending the central character.

THE WITCH (or BIRD, PLANE, FLY) WHO COULDN'T FLY could spur sympathetic storytellers into finding solutions to this dilemma. When a sobbing witch disturbs the spooky Halloween night air, a bat, a ghost, and a goblin join forces to fix her broken broom. Or perhaps in this age of technology brooms are antiquated, so that an inventor must create a special new mode of transportation for her.

THE INVISIBLE ____________ is a theme that captures the imagination. An invisible cat who has bred with another invisible cat has caused an invisible-cat epidemic in a city. The unison of meows terrifies the cityfolks, but nobody can catch the cats because nobody can see them. How are the cats caught? Is it by looking through special X-ray eyes or by splattering a highly visible spray paint everywhere?

There are, of course, many other approaches toward developing a conflict. *Brainstorming* with a team or group builds a storehouse of ideas from which to select. If the ideas are slow in coming, then ask specific questions to stimulate thought:

What are the unique characteristics of a rope? Of a ruler?
What would you do if you had a million dollars?

A GIANT DOG COLLAR

What problems might arise if you were rich?
What would you do if you were a witch?
What would you do if you were a witch who couldn't fly?
What would happen if you were invisible?
What new problems could being invisible bring?

By this point we've come a considerable distance in creating a story. We have sequenced events and introduced characters, thus creating *episodes*. We have related these events to a *theme* or idea. We created *conflicts* which catapult the story forward, as the characters encounter a difficulty or problem in the story. Now we have all the story-making ingredients at hand, except one. We must now resolve the tension, and devise a *climax* to the story. In so doing, we will reach the story's conclusion.

THE CLIMAX

The climax is the point in the story at which all the complications, both of characters and circumstances, have not only been introduced but have interacted in such a way as to move the story forward toward its inevitable conclusion. The climax is not the end of the story, but rather the highest peak of intensity after which we make the final run to the story's resolution.

It is important that the climax does not occur too early. Most climaxes occur near the end of the story, leading to a short downhill run. Thus in teaching students about such difficult concepts as conflicts and story climaxes, I prefer to have the students first plan or write their stories without any reference to these technical terms. Many children naturally incorporate these strategies into their stories, yet premature introduction of these concepts might inhibit the flow of ideas. Once the stories have been written, use them as examples to discuss the concepts of conflict and climax. Compare stories in order to show how varied the conflicts and climaxes of stories can be. You will find that working with the students' own material will give you more meaningful illustrations of these terms than examples taken from a book. Once the students understand these ideas, they should be given an opportunity to elaborate upon what they have learned.

If the method is taught in too structured a way, the participants concentrate on structure and form rather than letting their own natural, creative resources take the lead. Presenting the project (any project) in a loose format with *as few restrictions as possible* can produce surprisingly creative results. On the other hand, enough guidelines should be introduced to lay a foundation from which to work.

It is helpful, also, to discuss and compare ideas and stories developed within the group so that the members can learn from one another's successes and mistakes. Constant reinforcement is also necessary to encourage and perpetuate activity by the students. After they have written their own stories and evaluated them in a brainstorming session, have them rework the weak parts of the stories to improve the episodes, conflicts, and climax.

To insure an atmosphere in which this free exchange of ideas can flourish, set the tone from the very beginning. The students must know that you are receptive to their ideas and that you have full confidence in them. This confidence is the most critical factor in allowing creativity to prosper. Thus, when too much structure is imposed, the students sense a lack of trust in their own approach and ability; for the instructor this structure becomes a crutch with which to guarantee "safe" results. "Being safe" is not being creative. Both "right" and "wrong" answers are essential to creative thinking and learning.

Reaching a Climax by Building Up Episodes

Until now the climax of a story has been discussed in rather general terms. But how do we actually join the episodes of a story together in a pattern that leads up to a climax? The most skillfully planned stories are composed of linking episodes which create the effect of continually heightened adventure or anticipation. However the story itself begins, at some point near the opening, a series of episodes must begin to climb gradually to the climax. The preliminary planning of a story sketch can effectively help us order the events of the story, if we remember to be flexible at all times as we flesh out the story.

Here is a thumbnail sketch of *two cooks argue over the soup:*

OPENING

1. The cooks prepare the soup.
2. The cooks argue over whether to salt the soup or not.
3. The Boss serves the soup and fish to the customers.
4. A customer complains that the soup tastes terrible.
5. The Boss returns to the kitchen with the soup and fish.
6. The cooks labor again over the soup and argue further on whether to salt or not.

ORDERED BUILD-UP OF MIDDLE

7. The Boss serves the soup and fish to a second customer.
8. The second customer also complains, that the soup tastes terrible.
9. The Boss returns again to the kitchen with an ultimatum to the cooks to improve the soup—or else!
10. The cooks once again collaborate on refining the soup and whether to salt or not.
11. A full fledge battle occurs and the cooks are knocked out senseless.

	12. The fish solves the dilemma through cleverness.
ENDING	13. All is happy.

Or the story build-up might follow a less obvious pattern. Instead of a straight uphill climb it might alternate between high and low points, eventually rising to the ultimate climax. For example:

OPENING	1. The cooks prepare the soup.
HIGH POINT	2. The cooks argue over whether to salt the soup or not.
LOW POINT	3. The fish is served to the customers.
HIGH POINT	4. Havoc takes place among the customers.
LOW POINT	5. The fish escapes and finds refuge.
HIGH POINT	6. The fish encounters the cooks again and another argument occurs on whether to salt the soup or not.
	7. Full scale battle takes place.
LOW POINT	8. The fish evades the turmoil and finds a friend.
ENDING	9. The fish's dilemma is resolved through the friend and it lives happily ever after.

It is clear that high points are generally best achieved through the use of conflict, which can generate and prolong strong tension. Although such events as circuses, fanfares, fights and noisy celebrations are, in a sense, high points, they do not lend the strength to a story that a conflict does. Similarly, remember that it is not effective to unleash a full battle upon your audience, a battle for which they are not prepared. Take your time in letting a situation build to a crescendo. Children often insert fights and violence into a show without much intrinsic meaning, thus boring the audience while the characters senselessly battle on stage.

Work closely with the students to establish some sense of order and progression when a fight does occur. The puppets should not simply bat each other to death onstage, but significant action should build upwards. Refer to the cook episode on page 27 to illustrate this technique. Encourage the students, too, to add as much variety as possible to the fight itself. Have the children watch and discuss slapstick movie heroes, such as Charlie Chaplin, the Marx Brothers and the Keystone Cops. In so doing, they will learn how to expand upon an event or idea, gradually weaving it into a meaningful story.

Charlie Chaplin is the master artist in capitalizing upon and enlarging a small idea. The famous scene in Chaplin's *The Gold Rush,* during which he cooks and eats his own shoe, is perhaps an all-time masterpiece of effective build-up. Just as one would in a well-planned fight scene, Chaplin works up to the high point of the action gradually. The audience first begins to giggle and snicker sporadically, then more fully and finally reaches a level of laughter that has everyone rolling in the aisles. This build-up technique is a secret to which every storyteller should pay particular heed.

The Ending

For the audience, the end symbolizes a story told. There are as many ways to end a story as to begin one, but whatever idea is chosen it should be in harmony with the rest of the story. A clear concept of the theme or central idea of the story, as discussed earlier, will help tie together the entire story and prevent the ending from becoming a disjointed idea tacked on at the last. The ending finishes the "picture" and thereby leaves the audience with its last and most important impression of the story as a whole.

This last stroke should be a well-defined one that makes it very clear to the audience that the story is over. The ending could be as subtle as two characters hugging each other in friendship or as blunt as a final edict by a stern king. It could be as loud as a parade with a noisy band marching into the distance, or it could be as low-keyed as simply telling the moral of the story or leaving the audience with a question.

Brainstorming for an Ending

Just as in shaping the beginning and middle of a story, a brainstorming session is helpful in determining the ending. Here are some suggestions from brainstorming for an ending to *two cooks argue over the soup:*

—The fish suggests to the cooks that they go out among the customers and take a survey on whether to salt the soup or not. The cooks take a public poll in the Grand Dining Room, much to the surprise of the customers. It is decided after tallying the poll not to salt the soup and instead place giant salt shakers on the tables. The fish lives peacefully ever-after, swimming in circles in the big pot of bland soup, perpetually contributing its ancient flavor—without salt.

—A sweet old lady, who is one of the waiting customers, comes peeking into the kitchen to find the cooks unconscious and the fish in misery. She befriends the fish and listens patiently to its problems. She then dons cook's apron and spoon and starts attacking the soup and finds a solution to give the soup pungent flavor—a bag of lavender she carries around in her pocketbook. Upon remedying the soup the cooks wake and are extremely pleased with the flavor and their lavender soup. They agree to let the sweet old lady take the fish home to be her pet, to help her preoccupy her loneliness.

Using a narrator and dimming the lights are two techniques for indicating that a show is over. Techniques alone, however, are not enough; the ending must be a well-designed part of the story.

The Celebrated Ending

The end of a story or play is not a final termination, for within every ending are the seeds of many other beginnings. The ending is an author's statement of completion; it signifies that individual sequences have been transformed into a completed story. It is also the signal that now is the time to sow seeds for another beginning. In the words of Mark Twain, the creative process is a "giant vat" which, upon emptying, automatically fills up again. The creative act, in other words, knows no such thing as an absolute end. It is prolific because the more one creates the more one wishes to create; the vat becomes a bottomless pit.

Creativity does not come to us packaged as a gift; it is not something that we simply have or do not have. The crucial attribute is knowing how to train ourselves in the techniques needed to forge creative thought. First, we must be motivated and have the courage to try new ideas. Second, we must have stimuli and the freedom to be original. And third, to be creative we must persevere. As in other things, we work by trial and error, a process which often initiates a battle between frustration and failure on one side and success itself on the other. The creative person must be willing to accept all three—frustration, failure, and success—together.

But the reward for having harvested an original idea is so fine that it, in itself, becomes part of the celebration. A young man in Scotland, Richard Wawro, in spite of being classified mentally retarded, almost daily paints magnificent crayola pictures. Upon completing a picture, he tenderly burnishes it before presenting it to his father. At this point a ritual is performed. Richard and his father join hands and momentarily dance about the room in joy; it is their celebration of Richard's struggle. One does not need to perform such an overt act to share in this celebration of creativity—it is simply there; one senses it. Thus for the author, the end of the story is the time to plant more seeds to be harvested in yet another celebration—this, then, is the creative cycle.

Brainstorming

As the adage goes: Two heads are better than one. In creating a puppet story, brainstorming can trigger a flood of ideas with a single word, expanding the thought processes in ways not always possible by an individual, alone.

One of the greatest advantages of brainstorming is that it creates fellowship. A bond joins people in a group together who originate, respond and react to a mutual idea. It is a meaningful means of sharing both ideas and experiences. Furthermore, because it focuses on the whole more than on the parts, brainstorming helps to distract from the self-consciousness which often inhibits us from expressing creative ideas.

Almost any creative art or academic program can benefit from brainstorming sessions, especially when the sessions are alternated with projects designed for individual work. These two approaches can deeply enrich one another: Brainstorming encourages expansion; individual projects encourage depth and concentration.

No one in a brainstorming group should ever fear being ridiculed for *ANY* idea. It is imperative that each participant feel that his or her idea is worthy and belongs to the overall scheme of things, even if it is only in helping someone else come up with a better idea. For these reasons, it is good to begin a brainstorming session by explaining its purpose to the children: It is important to emphasize that *quantity,* rather than quality, is what the group seeks. Though ideas will not always seem like good ones at the time, it is most important that as many ideas be searched for and found as possible. We are expanding exponentially at this point. Later we will delve more deeply into single areas.

It is possible for a single person to hold a brainstorming session with him- or herself. In this case, one should write down every idea that comes to mind, and then examine each as to its viability. In addition to the *individual level,* sessions may be on *team and group* levels as well. In fact, team and group levels are more commonly the case. A team should be relatively small to function well, normally no more than three or four members. A group may be as large as the leader can comfortably handle without losing the intimacy that is crucial to any brainstorming session.

Brainstorming to Create a Story

—*Start with the group.* Developing a story with students may involve

brainstorming on all three levels. For example, story development could begin as the group (not yet divided into teams) searches for key words and images from which to derive a story. Start by writing a particular theme (such as Christmas, Love, George Washington, Summer, the Desert, Pollution) on the blackboard in order to spark ideas. Ask the group to express any word or image that comes to mind.
For example, here are some themes with words and images they might trigger:

THEME	**WORDS AND IMAGE**
Christmas	—love; Santa Claus; snow; giving, tinsel; going for a visit; I want a robot doll; make cookies; excited; can't wait; down the chimney
Pollution	—cars; coughing; animals suffer; I hate litter; fumes; let's do something about it; concerned

Continue until you feel you have extracted as many words as possible or until the students appear to tire of this technique. The group will soon have covered the blackboard with a long list of words. Now have the children select the words or images they like best and ask them to develop some idea-sentences around which to build a story. For example:

THEME	**WORDS AND IMAGES**	**IDEA-SENTENCES**
Christmas	*Tinsel*	—There is a shortage of tinsel and the characters open their own tinsel factory. —A tinsel thief comes around to steal all the tinsel. —The story takes place in Tinsel-land with strange tinsel people.

THEME	**WORDS AND IMAGES**	**IDEA-SENTENCES**
Pollution	*I hate litter.*	—A sweet lady turns bitter because of too much litter. (Showing how pollution can affect our personalities.) —Have a contest between an "I love litter" and "I hate litter" character. (End up with a winner and a grand prize). —Solve the litter problem in an imaginary town through an unusual concerned citizens group.

(This technique of using a theme to formulate an idea-sentence may be used as effectively in individual and team brainstorming sessions as well.)

—*Divide into teams.* Once the members of the group have shared ideas and stimulated their imaginations, you may form teams of two or four individuals so that each team can develop its own story. Each team would then write out its story, piecing together events and characters based upon the idea-sentence, theme, words and images, which it chose as a group.

Since each child will have only one puppet (unless time permits more), the number of story characters might be limited to the size of the team. This limitation might help simplify the production but is not necessary, since additional or secondary characters (such as a choral group, a flying cupid, or a bird) can quickly be assembled from figures drawn on cardboard and manipulated on a rod.

In general, the only criterion for the children to follow is that they create stories with a *beginning, a middle, and an end.* Older students may be asked to think specifically about the climax and the conflict involved in their stories. With any age level, however, it may be less restricting to bring up these details *after* the children have written a preliminary story outline for which you can present actual examples. Do not encourage script writing at this point because it, too, inhibits the free flow of ideas at this early stage of development. If you want a script, develop it after the story is completed.

—*Work again with the group.* Before writing a script, if you choose to do so, let the children return once more to the group for a brainstorming session. They can, then, share their stories and improve upon them with input from the group. Whether the children will continue working as a group or return to their teams depends upon the particular goal desired:

—Each team might incorporate the suggestions given its story and begin working on the finished puppet production in order to present it to the group or to another audience.

—The group might decide to present only one story, to be chosen by casting votes for the best team effort. (With this in mind, the stories could include larger casts.) The individual members of the group could then be assigned various functions to complete the story presentation, such as outline or script writing, making the puppets, building the scenery and props, planning the sound and special effects, choosing the music, and handling the publicity. One member of the group or an adult leader could act as director.

—It might be decided instead to use several stories, perhaps three out of six that were developed. The group could vote upon which of these stories to use, and then assemble them into a short-story series, perhaps with a puppet emcee or live moderator tying the parts of the presentation together.

Carol Sterling, an art teacher from New Jersey, and a wiz in brainstorming techniques, is responsible for having taught me what I know about brainstorming, many thanks!

Improvisational Puppet Plays

Improvisational puppet plays are great fun for all ages and provide their own special rewards. First, improvisation frees the performer from the word-for-word script and resultant mechanical performances which often occur from such scripts. Such improvisational acting allows one to think and act "with the puppet" rather than merely repeat words by rote. This spontaneous thinking process, shared with the puppet, enables the performer to unify action and dialogue simultaneously in such a way as to gauge the audience's reaction and respond to it.

Second, improvisation gives the performers an open-ended freedom, such as is not available in formal scripts, in creating and expressing ideas as the story unfolds. With this freedom no two rehearsals are ever the same, thus preventing boredom from repetitive rehearsals.

Third, an improvisational outline is less time-consuming to create than a formal script. It is an excellent method for quickly developing a story with a group when only limited time is available. It is also appropriate for a long-term project which evolves into a fully polished production.

Handling an improvisational outline requires neither more nor fewer skills than a written script does, but rather different skills, skills which will materialize through practice, sensitivity, and careful observation during rehearsals. The role of the director/leader during rehearsals will vary; if the improvisational outline is merely thought of as a brief exercise, then the leader takes a fairly passive role, letting the group perform at an informal-play level with only minimal direction. If, on the other hand, the project is a more ambitious one, the leader must act more strongly as a coach and mediator in full control at all times. The leader in this instance is a catalyst, lengthening or shortening parts as needed to hasten the transformation of the parts into a unified whole.

Suggestions for conducting a first improvisational run-through:

—Be sure all the players are fully briefed on the story outline prior to the run-through. Tack up a copy of the outline backstage so that the players can refer to it.

—Organize the players backstage in order of appearance during the performance, so that they will enter and exit smoothly. Plan ahead as

to which hands to use, and arrange the puppets accordingly.
—Stand or sit frontstage, close to the stage opening, with the outline in hand.
—Give a signal for the performers to begin, letting them simply move into the show.
—Follow the outline in a loose fashion, concentrating at this point on blocking out a correct sequencing of the entrances and exits of each character.
—Let the characters talk freely as the sequencing occurs. The rehearsal may be awkward at first, depending upon how much of a "ham" each player is.
—Prompt or direct the performers only as necessary. When the production seems bogged down, turn to the group for advice; not only does this technique relieve the director from having to solve all the problems but it contributes additional ideas to the story as well.

1) If someone is shy or struggling for words, stop the show and ask questions that help elicit dialogue. For example: What is it like to be a fish constantly in the midst of cooks, arguing? What would you say if you were a mad/sad fish?
2) Sometimes a performer doesn't need stimulus to free-associate but instead talks too much. If the dialogue begins to drag on to the point of boredom, again stop the show. This time ask questions about how the dialogue could be concentrated.

—Allow sufficient practice time. Any first or second run-through of an improvisational skit will seem awkward and choppy. If you want a polished, formal performance, then you will have to extend the rehearsal time accordingly; the exact time required will vary according to the skills of the performers and director.

After a sequencing pattern is understood, it is more important to concentrate on rehearsing the parts rather than the whole. Each episode should be fully developed. (The group can expand episodes by employing the brainstorming sessions mentioned earlier, if necessary.) If each episode can stand on its own, then accomplishing a smooth production is only a matter of tying the entire story together through sequencing once again during the last few rehearsals.

Some drama games or experiences would be useful before beginning improvisation.
Several good books available are: *Making Puppets Come Alive* by Larry Engler and Carol Fijan; *Development Through Drama* by Brian Way; and *Theater Games* by Viola Spolin.

The Story Outline

An outline is useful in constructing story plot. Serving as both a guide for improvisational puppet shows and also as a basis for formal scripts, an outline provides an abbreviated sketch of the basic events of the story. Accordingly it should be kept fairly simple and include the sequential action of the story, as well as important details. At the same time it should remain flexible, subject to change when new ideas surface. When working with children on improvisational puppet shows, leave spaces in the outline for jotting down notes during rehearsals with tips for the final production.

To illustrate, here is a sample story outline for the play derived from the original expanded episode *two cooks argue over the soup* which was detailed earlier:

Sample Story Outline

Title—A Salty Tale

What It Is About—This is a story about how disagreement causes upheaval, and its effect upon others.

Characters—

1. Leo (*first cook*)
2. Joe (*second cook*)
3. Fish
4. Boss
5. Dignified Gentleman (*customer*)
6. Witty Lady (*customer*)
7. President of City National Bank

SCENE I:

Setting and Time—It is dinner time inside the busy kitchen of an exclusive restaurant. Pots and pans are in disarray everywhere.

The Events—

Leo stirs the soup to the beat of combo music.
Leo tastes the soup.
Leo decides to add vital ingredients to the soup.
A fish pops out of the soup and squirts Leo in the eye.
Joe comes over to taste the soup.
Joe says the soup needs salt.
Leo disagrees and confers with the fish; they decide the soup does not need salt.
An argument occurs between Leo and Joe over whether to salt or not to salt.
The argument turns into a full-scaled battle. Both Leo and Joe are knocked senseless.
The Boss enters and yells, "The customers are waiting!"
The Boss in desperation, whisks up the fish and places it on

a platter to serve to the customers.

SCENE II:
Setting and Time—In the Grand Dining Room.
The Events—

The fish is served to a dignified gentleman.
The gentleman prepares himself to eat the fish.
The fish jumps off the plate into the gentleman's lap.
The gentleman shrieks and runs out the door.
The Boss then serves the same fish to a witty lady.
The witty lady prepares to eat the fish.
When she is not looking, the fish jumps off the plate and hides in the witty lady's pocketbook.
The witty lady is upset when she discovers the fish is gone. She accuses the Boss of insufficient service and hits him on the head with her pocketbook, as she exits.

SCENE III:
Setting and Time—Later, at the office of the City National Bank.
The Events—

The fish, still in the pocketbook, arrives at the office where the witty lady works.
While the witty lady begins work, the fish finds the opportunity to crawl out of the pocketbook, and into the bank president's office.
The president sees the fish and decides it is just what he needs for a big banquet.
The president calls the exclusive restaurant to send over two of their best cooks to prepare the banquet.
Leo and Joe arrive, with pots and pans clanging.
The cooks are surprised to see the fish again.
Back in the soup the fish goes!
Again the argument begins over whether to salt the soup or not.
Another battle takes place and again Leo and Joe are knocked unconscious.
The fish is now very sad, living in such constant turmoil.
The witty lady befriends the fish and decides it should live in the office aquarium. Because of its amazing age, it becomes a remarkable showpiece and people come from miles around to see it.

Developing a Story with Children

Writing a story, regardless of the length, often poses difficulty for children. While they are extremely adept at originating clever ideas, they are generally weak in expanding these ideas into full, well-rounded stories; as a result, their story plots are often too brief and drastically underdeveloped. The use of brainstorming techniques and special exercises on expanding idea sentences (as mentioned on page 27) can cultivate the student's prowess at storywriting.

Create an entire story with the students, by first holding a brainstorming session from which you can construct a sample story frame outline on the black board. Ask specific questions in the following order so that students understand the sequencing which is important in constructing a story:

—*What are the characters?* The characters may be of the students' own creations, such as with the abstract puppets on page 106. Or perhaps they are characters which the leader has specifically chosen to create a challenge—such unlikely characters as an anteater, a professor, and an octopus; or a smiling lady, a grouchy elephant, and a snake.
—*What is the setting?* Where the story takes place sets the tone and mood, and thereby lays the foundation for the story to follow. Will it be on a college campus, in a South American jungle, or underwater? Have the students explore the setting to determine how it will affect the story.
—*What happens first?* Ask students about alternative ways the story might open. What characters will be involved in the beginning? What will they say and do?
—*What happens next?* Develop a series of happenings as shown previously for *two cooks argue over the soup.* Repeat the question "What happens next?" until a satisfactory chain of events has been constructed.
—*How does the story end?* Have the students discuss alternative endings before deciding, as a class, upon the final one.
—*What is the story about?* Now the children may discuss the moral or the essence of the story.
—*What is the title of the story?* Discovering an appropriate title after the story frame outline is developed, rather than before, allows more flexibility to change the story while it is being developed.

The Script

A script offers both advantages and disadvantages. As an aid in teaching students written and oral language skills, a script brings forward excellent motivation. It is much more fun to work on a project that will be performed than one which will be merely graded and filed away. On the other hand, it can serve as a hindrance to spontaneity in story performance. Children, especially those under eight, perform best with just a simple story outline and proper guidance. Concentrating upon reading the script can often cause a child to perform mechanically, neglecting what the puppets are doing and saying. Older students, however, often feel more comfortable with a written script and take pride in applying their language skills toward a more structured professional production. I prefer improvisational story outlines to scripts; however, the choice depends upon the individual's preferences and goals.

I recommend experimenting with both written and improvisational techniques. The *written script* requires additional rehearsals in order to overcome the potentially mechanical effect of the script. An *improvisational story outline* is a less structural format and thus permits greater flexibility and spontaneity on the part of both children and teacher. However, it also places more stringent demands upon the teacher. Students often fluctuate between being utterly shy or totally garrulous; it is the teacher's role to encourage the reticent and restrain the others.

Whether you choose a written script or an improvisational story outline, the key things to remember are to:

1) *think short;* 2) *think simple;* and 3) *think contrast and variety.*

Thinking Short

The story—For the novice, especially, it is better to aim for a well-made story of five to fifteen minutes rather than a mediocre longer one. A short format allows quality, with story development skills being stressed. If a longer production is desired, simply plan a show with two or three skits, instead of trying to stretch out a shorter one.

The dialogue—Keep the dialogue short. Too many shows, both amateur and professional, are plagued by superfluous dialogue. Puppets are not static dolls; rather, they are animated moving beings who speak as much with their bodies as with their mouths. A puppet standing in one place too long, delivering a long speech, is apt to bore the audience—

remember that losing the audience for even a moment can destroy the power of the performance. Aim at keeping the dialogue as short and meaningful as possible. In preparing the production, plan as much (or more) action into the play as there is dialogue.

Thinking Simple

Think simple in every aspect—dialogue, number of characters, scenery and scene changes, props, sound, and special efforts. Effort, time and skill should be wisely invested to develop a story with strength in its simplicity.

The characters—It is better to plan too few characters than too many. An audience enjoys getting to know a few characters in depth rather than an army of puppets superficially. Puppets marching on and off stage without any real purpose become tedious. If characters must be grouped—such as a herd of animals, a crowd, or a regiment of soldiers—bring them on en masse and consider treating them as a unit. Remember, too, that superfluous characters can cause confusion backstage as well as onstage. To reduce confusion, it is advisable to have no more than two or three puppeteers backstage at once; therefore, plan accordingly and have no more than three or four characters on stage at any one time.

The scenery and props—Struggling with frequent complicated scenery changes can easily disrupt the continuity of a performance. A few suggestive props or scene parts, such as a tree, house, or blue sky with a cloud, may be enough to fill the story's needs. While the audience usually enjoys scene changes, you should keep the scenery simple enough so that maneuvering does not become a chore. Long intermissions due to tedious scenery changes are another hazard to avoid. Intermissions as well as the story should be brief, because an audience forced to wait too long between acts soon becomes restless.

Thinking Contrast and Variety

The secret of any successful work of art—whether it be film, musical score, painting or puppet show—is *contrast and variety.* Striking contrast in all parts of the show helps make the work a success.

The story—A good story contains changing episodes which reflect a variety of moods. Walt Disney's *Bambi* is a perfect example of a master artist creating powerful mood changes: A quiet scene is a prelude to a suspenseful one; a happy song and dance are juxtaposed with a frightening scene. It is not necessary, of course, to include the entire spectrum of mood changes in a production, but it is advisable to change mood two or three times within a simplified work. A show that begins on a tender note may have a middle of drama and high suspense, ending once again on a tender note. Remember that a show which depicts all tenderness or all drama throughout cannot be a very interesting one.

The dialogue and action—Dialogue and action should be considered and planned simultaneously during script writing. Ask yourself, for example, such questions as: How do the dialogue and action arrange themselves? Are they patterned with enough variety to hold the interest of the audience? The following approaches to *two cooks argue over the soup* illustrate the importance of contrast in dialogue and action. First, a poor example:

JOE: Is that soup ready yet, Leo?
LEO: No, not yet, give it time.
JOE: But the Boss is getting angry.
LEO: You know I am striving for quality.
JOE: But the customers are waiting for the soup.
LEO: Patience is a virtue.

Now compare this to a better example:

JOE: Is that soup ready yet, Leo? The Boss is getting angry. (*Sniff, sniff*) Blah! That smells terrible! (*Takes a taste*) Ugh! And it tastes just as bad. Blah! Murder, just murder! You call that soup? What's in it anyway?
LEO: A lot of delicate ingredients and one very cooperative fish.
JOE: Let me see. (*Bends over the soup when fish appears and squirts him in the eye.*) Hey! Cut that out! (*Trues to catch fish and falls into the enormous pot of soup.*) Help! I can't swim! (*He paddles around to splashing sounds.*)
LEO: Here, take my hand!

Here we see the difference in the two approaches. The former follows a consistent pattern monotonously throughout the entire skit. The staccato effect of the predominantly short sentences is not an interesting one. The latter version strives for variety. Longer and shorter sentences are arranged with action between dialogue, and there is variety in punctuation as well as in dialogue and action. The second example, with its definite lack of sameness, makes a more interesting performance than the first example.

The characters—A gathering of people who all appear to look, think and talk alike would be dull, so, too, with a cast of puppets. A show of characters with heads all made from, say, the same round styrofoam balls would be far less interesting than one in which the characters have different forms and proportions. Observe people in a crowd. Which ones stand out as the most interesting to you? Perhaps a huge fat lady is chatting with a small thin man; a tall gangly lad is speaking with a beautiful young lady; a squarish chunky man is talking to a bookish, frail gentleman. With puppets we have the liberty to exaggerate these characteristics to the limit. After all, puppets are an exaggeration of reality —a puppet may be extremely tall, preposterously fat, or ridiculously small. Puppets can also be what people cannot. A puppet can have no neck whatsoever, funnel-like ears, or perhaps eyes at the back of the head. Despite the fact that puppets' characteristics are usually inspired by human ones, puppetry is most successful when it does not try to duplicate what real people can be and do. In other words, it thrives on the absurd.

The puppet's voice is also part of the character's contrast. When voices are too similar, it is hard to differentiate which voice belongs to which puppet. Experiment with voices. Contrast a grumbly low voice with a higher squeaky one; a smooth baritone with a hysterical tenor; or a sleepy, slow voice with one which is rapid fire. Any idiosyncracy in a puppet's personality, voice, or style of dialogue may contribute to the contrast within a play. A puppet may have a peculiar accent, continually rub its jaw or yawn in everyone's presence. Perhaps it walks with a strange gait or uses a unique phrase, such as Winnie the Pooh's "Oh, bother!" or Scrooge's "Bah, humbug!"

Another, perhaps more subtle, area of contrast is in the grouping pattern of the puppets' appearances onstage. For example, if three characters are constantly seen together throughout a show, the repetitive grouping pattern can soon become a bore. The grouping within a show should be varied—perhaps one character appears at times, two at others, and three at still another. Our eyes react in greater ways than we realize to such pattern contrast. Thus it is a treat to watch a production of Agatha Christie's *Ten Little Indians* because of the clever grouping of the ten characters in the play. At first only two characters appear, then one, then perhaps another two, then three. Later they are seen in varied groups of six, eight, and at times ten. Whether you are planning a story that involves two or ten characters, keep this important criterion of contrast in mind.

CHARACTER DEVELOPMENT

A puppet play owes part of its success to character identification, by the audience. The audience needs to relate to the characters, to care in some way about what happens to them. Creating an appealing, entertaining puppet is relatively simple, but presenting this puppet in such a way as to make the audience care about him is a skill that needs to be learned and developed. Of all the skills needed to produce a show, it is perhaps one of the most crucial for it is often a certain character who leaves a lasting impression on the audience rather than the work itself.

A recent production of *Little Red Riding Hood,* put on by Roberta Vest, Amburn Power and Fay Welch of the Athens Puppet Theater in Athens, Georgia, taught me the importance of this character identification. Their shaggy, nitwitted wolf was not the stereotypical malicious wolf we always think of; it was half pretense (a bit of the lion in *The Wizard of Oz*) and half tease, with a sense of humor that was absolutely winning. Captivating the entire audience, the wolf played the leading part in this interpretation, the character for whom the audience waited and the one who tied the entire production together. In another version, perhaps Little Red Riding Hood might be elected to play this central role.

How does one elicit this strong identity with a given character? First, one must have time, *time* within the play for the character not only to appear but to develop; time for the audience to become acquainted and emotionally involved with the character, to follow its adventures and care about its ultimate success. This character is seen often throughout the play and helps to link it together. Adept expansion of episodes which feature this central character helps pull the audience into a deeper level of involvement.

The second requirement is to develop a *strong personality* within the

LITTLE RED RIDING HOOD, by the Athens Puppet Theater

character. Very simply, this can be accomplished with outward gestures and distinctive voice quality. These traits can emphasize aspects of the character's personality, such as shyness, or mischief or wickedness. Or they may emphasize idiosyncrasies in the personality, developed specifically to enhance certain facets of the personality. Consider "Sneezy" or "Dopey" in the Disney version of *Snow White and the Seven Dwarfs* or Jim Henson's famous Sesame Street characters like *"Oscar the Grouch"* or *"Big Bird."* Whichever characteristics you decide to emphasize, it is critical that you remain consistent throughout the show.

The audience cannot identify with too many characters at once; therefore, choose one or two central characters and let the rest be of secondary importance. These remaining characters may have seperate personalities of their own, but they should be de-emphasized to enhance the effect of the whole. They should instead play a subsidiary role which buoys up the lead personalities by engaging contrasting or complementary attributes.

THE FORMAL SCRIPT

As in creating any other work of art, whether a painting or music or a piece of sculpture, writing a script should be a reflection of personal expression. Personal expression is the inner core of creativity, the golden nugget for which we search in every creative endeavor. If we concentrate first upon personal expression and second upon a well-written script—in just that order of priority—then we are working toward a worthy creative goal.

What *does* comprise a personal style? It is a style with which you feel harmony and one which you intuitively sense within yourself. It is not one that is borrowed from another author; therefore, although I would certainly like to write like A. A. Milne and to have achieved what he has with the indefatigable *Winnie the Pooh,* the fact is that I am not Milne. I am myself, an entirely different individual with an entirely different set of experiences and talents. It is these factors I must explore in order to discover who I am. What are my real feelings about things? How do I perceive my world? (Not Milne's or anyone else's.) How do I respond to the world? And how do I wish to share this world with others?

I am a nutshell with a nut inside. I may wish to protect my inner kernel from criticism, ridicule, or possible rejection, and therefore I may hide this inner kernel from others. However, such protection is harmful to both myself and others in terms of creativity output. In order to create something of worth, I must expose myself and risk vulnerability. Only in this way can I express what I truly feel.

In actually writing the script, first focus upon a subject about which you have feelings and opinions, whether it be the protection of wildlife, how to utilize leisure time or a grand political issue such as communism vs. capitalism. Exploring your ideas and feelings produces material that may be developed into a script. The style of the script itself must then take form. The style reflects the author's personality.

Authors such as A. A. Milne or Dr. Seuss have distinctive creative styles that definitely come from their inner core; both authors are difficult to duplicate because they represent the unique voices of individuals. Each of us is also unique and possesses our own inner core. Many fail because they deal only with words and nothing else. Words alone are not a story; ideas, feelings, and personality are the story, waiting to be discovered within us.

The script of each story-creator will differ, since each one is infused with the author's distinctive voice. But at the same time, authors should consider certain aspects in the process of developing a script: action and dialogue, surprises within the script; and evaluation of the script.

The Action

Whether you have chosen to present a classic fairy tale or a story entirely of your own making, a crucial element of your production is the action that it contains. Static puppets gabbing throughout a show have difficulty holding the attention of the audience, especially an audience of young children. Because we are beings who take great pleasure in both our auditory and visual senses, we lose a degree of totality from any experience in which one of these senses is deprived. Therefore, a puppet show should tantalize us with both visual and auditory delights in order to more fully stimulate the senses.

Learning to write action and gestures into the script is important for enriching any puppet play. Here are some guidelines for the use of action:

Use plenty of action. One of the chief benefits of a puppet's performing an action is that it can build up anticipation or tension and suspense. A puppet sneaking around, peering under beds and peeking into closets with spooky background music is much more suspenseful than a puppet saying, "I wonder what's under that bed" or "Hmmmm, I know there must be something in that closet." Such superfluous dialogue leaves little for the audience's imagination to ponder. Action, on the other hand, engages the audience's attention fully in the puppets' activity. A handy rule to follow when developing a script is: *Do not have the puppets speak when they can show.* Words can become a crutch for the playwright who fears the audience will not understand the actions of the puppets. Instead of relying upon this prop, boldly challenge the audience and yourself. With practice and constant evaluation of your work, you can create action segments which are an integral part of your story.

Keep the action moving. Watch successful children's programs to learn the secrets of effective action stories. Action prevents the story from stagnating and becoming bogged down. A well-designed story should flow from one action and dialogue section to the next. If you find your puppet freezing in one spot for a prolonged time, reevaluate your script to avoid such occurrences. If a lengthy dialogue should be necessary, remember that activity and dialogue may accompany and even enhance one another. There is no reason for a puppet not to be picking up toys or sweeping the floor, for example, while talking.

Enlarge the action. Because puppets are small creatures, they require extra large, exaggerated movements and gestures in order to be recognized by an audience, especially in a large room. Do not be afraid to experiment. A grand sweep of the puppet's hand can be more effective at times than a subtle movement. A puppet hanging over the front edge of the stage and weeping hysterically may be preferable to one that is softly sobbing. A leap across the stage might be more exciting than a straightforward walk.

Contrast subtleties with the action. At other times, try letting the subtleties and finer techniques of acting predominate. Use subtle and exaggerated action to add pronounced contrast to the show. In the case of the unstoppable hiccups, for example, begin with small, barely noticeable hiccups. Gradually build up to larger ones, then to still larger ones, and finally to huge ridiculous ones that throw the puppet spasmodically about the stage.

The Surprises

Puppets can do things that live actors can not. Use this crucial aspect of puppetry to best advantage. Puppet productions which merely imitate live shows tend to be uninteresting. Puppets have the gift of the absurd —they can jump higher and weep louder than can people; they can grow ridiculously tall, twist into pretzel shapes, fly through the air, or split in two. Take advantage of the puppets' special powers. Whether your approach is subtle or outrageous, search your imagination and grab bag of tricks to delight your audience. For example:

—what appears to be a small innocent spider is actually the mustache of a hidden but notorious big bad wolf;
—a small flower slowly grows into a walking monster;
—a sun rises, becoming increasingly more animated with a talking mouth and dancing sun rays;
—a dog's tail or person's nose grows to absurd lengths;
—a box has a bottomless pit from which things are pulled;
—a puppet turns around to reveal another face on the other side (perhaps a sad and a happy side);
—a handkerchief has a head put on it and comes to life, in full view of the audience.

Writing a Script for Children

In writing a script for children, never underestimate the natural intelligence of the children! Do not preach or become didactic in a puppet show! If a story is designed to educate, let it do so in a more subtle manner, with humor, interesting dialogue, and action.

The following script excerpts will clearly illustrate the difference between a dull, stilted text and one with a more interesting approach. First, the dull text:

CAROL: Hi, boys and girls. My name is Carol and I'm here to tell you about electricity. Won't you be smart after you hear what I have to say? Here is a book and today I'm going to read to you all about electricity.

JOHN: Hi, Carol. What are you doing?

CAROL: Oh, everybody, I want you to meet my friend John. It is good to see you, John. I'm going to tell the boys and girls about electricity.

JOHN: What's electricity?

CAROL: Electricity is very important. It is a form of energy that we use to help do work for us. Almost everybody uses electricity in some way.

JOHN: Where does electricity come from?

CAROL: That is a very good question, John. You must be very smart to ask questions like that. Let me read what the book has to say. It says that electricity is an electric current generated by a machine. That electricity is caused by . . . .

slowly make boy appear
a little boy is actually a fat boy
two lovely flowers turn into the paws of a horrible creature

THE SURPRISES

attach a balloon to a length of plastic tubing with masking tape; blow other end for expanding nose or body

seperate hand prop
a mischievous man waves with what appears to be an ultra long arm
a candy cane is actually a snake

THE SURPRISES

Compare the dialogue above with this more imaginative approach:

CAROL: (Pops up.) Hi!
JOHN: (Pops up.) Hi, Carol! What are you up to?
CAROL: Oh, Hi, John. I'm busy.
JOHN: Doing what?
CAROL: Studying this lamp. Isn't it remarkable?
JOHN: What do you mean? It's just an old lamp!
CAROL: Yes, but the light—it's so bright! Have you ever wondered what it would be like without electricity?
JOHN: Humm. No, I never thought about that. I guess it would be pretty dark, hum? Spooky maybe.
CAROL: Just a second! (Goes down for book, props it up, and starts to turn pages. She gets her nose caught in the book.) Hellp!
JOHN: (Helps her.)
CAROL: E-lec-tri-ci-ty . . . wow!
JOHN: What does it say?
CAROL: Too much! Are you sure you want to know?
JOHN: Of course!
CAROL: (Slams book shut and puts it down below.) I'll show you! (She pantomimes and builds a mock generator that produces sparks.)

1) The first script is altogether too wordy and on the whole quite static. The second script has a much faster pace and shows, rather than tells, what it's trying to teach.
2) The characters in the second script are introduced quite briefly. To avoid wordiness, their names are mentioned only once.
3) The second script does not state what the story is about, but lets it unravel naturally. It allows the audience to discover the story's content rather than merely state it. In this case we are led into the subject of electricity by the simple use of a lamp prop.
4) The first script contains superfluous sentences which should be avoided. "Won't you be smart?" is condescending to children over six years old, while "Let me see what the book has to say" is superfluous because it states what can easily be shown and assumed.
5) The first script "preaches"; the second script "shows" what electricity is all about, presenting a far more interesting and meaningful visual impression of the subject matter.

The Evaluation of the Script

Be ready to make changes. Even after compiling the formal script, remain flexible for changes at all times, even up to the moment of the final performance. Not until the first actual run-throughs of the show will the author be able to determine if any major changes are necessary, such as simplifying a complicated action, reordering the characters' entrances and exits, expanding an idea that is weak, etc. Remember that the first rehearsal is often extremely awkward and choppy. Therefore, before considering any major changes be sure that they are not simply a result of unfamiliarity with the story. A second or third run-through will give you more familiarity to better determine where changes should actually be made.

Trim wordiness. In reviewing your overall script, scrutinize it carefully for superfluous words and eliminate them. Is there unnecessary dialogue or action that adds little to the overall story? Streamline sentences and paragraphs in order to avoid wordiness. Look over your script and read it aloud, word by word. Is it too talky? Does one sentence repeat the same thought expressed in another one? Does a particular sentence say what the action had already shown?

One of the hardest things for a playwright to do is to take out a segment of a completed story, particularly a good one. It is essential that one learns early to accept such necessities. One of the worst things a playwright can do is to let an entire production suffer because of sections which should have been deleted. It may be that such a segment simply has nothing to do with the rest of the story, or that it is superfluous and slows down the action of the whole. Deletions and other such revisions should be viewed as sacrifices of the parts for the good of the whole work. A good playwright is one who constantly remodels ideas in conjunction with rehearsals, reevaluating the parts while keeping sight of the whole.

Summary of How to Create a Good Script

1) Work with a good plot, a simple story line, excitement, humor and action.
2) Create a strong visual impression of the plot. Learn to visualize puppets, scenery, and props when writing the script.
3) Work with simplicity in *all* aspects of the show.
4) Avoid long speeches; instead use economical dialogue and action.
5) Keep the story moving at a good pace. Don't be afraid to eliminate parts that make the story drag.
6) Strive for contrast, variety, and surprise.
7) Develop an opening that captivates, a middle that sustains and an ending that impresses.
8) Work toward personal expression and style.

A SALTY TALE

A sample script based on the expanded idea sentence *two Cooks Argue Over the Soup.*

SCENE I

CHARACTERS—

Leo (*first cook*)
Joe (*second cook*)
Fish
Boss
Dignified Gentleman (*customer*)
Witty Lady (*customer*) Sensible Lady

SETTING AND TIME—

It is dinnertime inside the busy kitchen of an exclusive restaurant. Pots and pans are in disarray everywhere. An enormous pot of soup center stage.

LEO: (*Stirs soup with an oversized spoon, to the beat of combo music. Create steaming effect by squeezing baby powder*) Mumbo-jumbo, seafood gumbo. Mumbo, gumbo-seafood gumbo. Humph! It appears to be lacking something. (*Sniff, sniff*) Its aroma is just not what it should be. A superb soup should be one that is . . . ahhhh . . . tantalizing to the nose, (*Sniff, sniff*), and to the palate as well. (*He tastes the soup with a spoon*) Definitely not right! It's definitely not exquisite enough for the clientele of this fine restaurant. (*He opens refrigerator door and pulls out an immense bundle of vegetables to add to the soup*) Ahhhh . . . . what we need are ingredients of a refined nature to embellish this soup. (*Throws in an assortment of vegetables one-by-one, such as whole carrots, chunky potatoes, an overwhelming amount of parsley, turnips, etc. He stirs once again to the beat of combo music. Bubbles from a soap bubble-blower appear above the soup while he stirs*) *Sniff, sniff* (*He tastes the soup*) Absolutely not! It has no refinement, no subtleties whatsoever! Oh my, what am I ever going ot do? (*Wrings hands and paces floor*) I know! I forgot the secret ingredients! (*He turns around and produces an assortment of odd items—hats, gloves, jewelry, etc.—to throw in the soup.* (*Tastes*) *Aha, that's better!* (*Stirs again to combo music, then bends down to taste the soup when suddenly a fish pops up and squirts him in the eye*) Hey! (*He bends down and again gets squirted in the eye*) What is this nonsense? A fish in my soup! Are you trying to make a fool of a master cook!

FISH: Slurp, slurp, cookie.

LEO: What did you say?

FISH: Slurp, slurp, cookie:

LEO: No, you can't have a cookie. Now get back down there where you belong. (*Stirs again to combo music*) Gumbo, gumbo, seafood gumbo.

JOE: (*Appears from left stage*) Is that soup ready yet, Leo? The boss is getting angry. (*Sniff, sniff*) Blah! That smells terrible! (*Takes a taste*) Ugh! And it tastes just as bad. Blah! Murder, just murder! You call that soup? What's in it anyway?

LEO: A lot of delicate ingredients and one very cooperative fish.

JOE: Let me see. (*Bends over soup when fish appears and squirts him in the eye*) Hey! Cut that out! (*Tries to catch fish and falls into enormous pot of soup*) Help!, I can't swim! (*Splashing sounds while he paddles around*)

LEO: Here, take my hand! (*Pulls Joe out of soup*)

JOE: A bit wet in there. Hey! (*Reaches up to discover the fish under his hat*) Look at this! This is no ordinary fish. It looks like it's a hundred years old! No wonder the soup tasted terrible. (*Drops the fish into pot with a plunking sound*) Leo, you can't make soup with a hundred year old fish, it's just too tough. Now the soup's ruined and the boss will be mighty upset.

LEO: I think the soup tastes simply delicious. The fish gave it just the right touch. (*Tastes soup*) Ummm . . . smack, smack . . . ahhh . . . yumm . . . (*Makes sounds of culinary ecstasy*)

JOE: No, it's not edible this way. (*Tastes soup*) Blah! But I think . . . (*Pause*) . . . I think (*Scratches his head*) . . . yes, it will work! We can save it with salt. That's it, salt will save it.

LEO: Never! You know and I know that a good cook NEVER resorts to the use of salt. (*He confers with the fish who agrees that it doesn't need salt*)

JOE: But it's the only way.

LEO: NEVER! (*Stands in front of soup with arms folded in determination*) And the fish also says NEVER!

TO SALT OR NOT TO SALT?

JOE: Yes!

LEO: No!

JOE: Yes! (*Raps Leo over the head with his spoon*)

LEO: Ouch! No! Never! (*Picks up fish and flops Joe over the head with it*)

JOE: Ouch! Yes! (*Bangs the lid of a pot over Leo's head*)

LEO: Ouch! No! (*Raps Leo again with the fish*)

JOE: Ouch! Yes! (*Uses an array of pots and pans to pound Leo*)

LEO: Ohhhh . . . (*Falls senseless to the ground with a thud*)

JOE: Ohhhhh . . . (*With the last blow, he too falls to the ground with a thud*)

FISH: (*Pops up*) Oh, ohh . . . (*Gets two wet towels and puts them on Joe's and Leo's foreheads*) Oh, ohhh. Wakee up, wakee up, please wakee up! (*Fish speaks in high, squeaky voice*)

BOSS: (*Comes thumping in*) Customers are waiting! Customers are waiting! What are **YOU** two waiting for? Customers aren't going to wait all day. (*Sees cooks on the floor*) Get up! Now's no time for a nap. (*No response from cooks*) Did you hear me? Get up! Sleeping on the job, eh? For that, you're both fired. Did you hear me? I said YOU'RE FIRED! (*He sees fish*) What's this? (*Picks up the fish by tail*) Ahaa, this may save the day yet! (*He whisks the fish onto a platter and carefully places a sprig of parsley on top*) Perfect! It's a culinary's masterpiece! (*Majestically walks to the Grand Dining Room, delicately balancing platter, exit right.*)

Things to note: Script Evaluation

—*The patterns of dialogue and action are varied.* At times, as during the argument scene between Leo and Joe, there are short, staccato sentences. At other times, there are more complex sentences which add diversity to the script.

—*The punctuation is varied.*

—*Contrasts in the individual characters are incorporated in the script.* Leo, for example, has the characteristics of a refined cook from the old school. His vocabulary includes fitting words such as *aroma* and *exquisite.* Joe, on the other hand, contrasts Leo's refinements by presenting himself as a direct, less complicated personality. The fish, in spite of having the least dialogue, has strong audience appeal because of its naive and defenseless nature. These characteristics are magnified only because they are juxtaposed next to characteristics of opposing types.

When writing a script, I find it extremely helpful to actually have puppets nearby. I often pick one up and give it an appropriate voice as I write the script itself; in this way, the puppet helps to formulate its own distinctive language style. I continue to work on the characterization throughout the script, striving for consistency and for contrasts with the other characters.

—*Entrances and exits are written into the script.* (Note the left, right, top, or bottom appearances.)
—*Music, sound and special effects are included in the script.*
—*Each word and sentence should have significance.* Read a group of sentences over and over again, searching for words superfluous to the overall thought. For example, notice the difference in:

JOE—Help! I can't swim!
JOE—Help, this is terrible! I can't swim!

"This is terrible" is superfluous in that it only reinforces what the situation already implies.

LEO—Here, take my hand!
LEO—Here, take my hand, I'll pull you out.

"I'll pull you out" is redundant and says what is already being shown by the action. In considering the two examples above, a word or two deletion may seem trivial indeed, but when one considers the script as a whole, such superfluous passages will result in a show that is too long and becomes tedious.

Converting a Story from a Book into a Puppet Play

Schools and libraries abound with rich source material which is adaptable to puppet plays. Well-known folk tales and popular contemporary children's stories are ready choices for story conversion. However, it is also great fun to explore some of the less familiar stories found in the library's bookshelves. Legends from China and Russia, Indian and Eskimo lore, European and Japanese folk tales are among the best of sources.

The ideal story to be turned into a play has only a few characters and an uncomplicated plot. It moves along at an even, steady pace and is balanced between dialogue and action. (Milne's *Winnie the Pooh* stories are a script-finder's dream, in that they offer prewritten dialogue for the characters. *The Bear's Vacation* by Stan and Jan Berenstein; *Alexander and the No Good, Horrible, Very Bad Day* by Judith Viorst and the *Tale of Peter Rabbit* by Beatrix Potter are other good examples of stories with balanced dialogue and action.)

Stories vary greatly, and finding the ideal story is almost like searching for the ideal person; it simply doesn't exist. Therefore the key to story adaptation is the ability to adjust. Since stories are not written with puppet plays in mind, wit and adaptability are required to "make a story work." In general the creator of a puppet play must learn to shorten, lengthen, add on and take out as needed. Above all, one need not adhere rigidly to any story.

1) *Stories with short or weak central plots* need to be expanded in order to be used as a puppet presentation. For example, *Little Red Riding Hood* is a tale with an exceedingly short central plot. According to the original version, Little Red Riding Hood dashes through the woods, briefly encounters the wolf, and continues on to Grandmother's house. The playwright may choose to embellish the woods scene by adding characters and dialogue, elements of weather and nature, drama and excitement.

2) *Stories with too much dialogue,* on the other hand, need condensing. A story such as Dr. Seuss' *Cat in the Hat* has much dialogue that would be superfluous in a play. For the play's effectiveness, the dialogue should be shortened and the action pursued instead.

3) *Narrated stories* are good approaches. Some books naturally seem to lend themselves best to being read aloud by a narrator who is in front or back stage while the puppets act out the story. Such examples include Dr. Seuss' *Cat in the Hat* and Slobadkin's *Caps for Sale.*

4) *Stories with no dialogue* (or hardly any) are also delightful, such as *The Last Free Bird* by A. Harris Stone or *Skates* by Ezra Jack Keats. Producing one of these stories would certainly be a challenge to any novice—or professional—puppeteer! In such a case, the performers might use a simple musical score to create the backdrop for action. On the whole, the performers would strengthen the production by learning to concentrate on meaningful action, movement, and gestures.

New Approaches to Old Ideas

An idea that older students particularly enjoy is writing *spoofs or new twists* to familiar fairy tales and nursery rhymes. Often presented with humor, these versions can give a fresh outlook to old tales. One of my most successful shows was a conversion of *Little Red Riding Hood* into *Little Red Riding Mouse,* in which all the characters except the bad wolf were mice. Or the entire story could be placed in a city setting, with skyscrapers instead of trees, a wolf in a business suit, and a granny who lives in a penthouse apartment; certainly city children would readily identify with such a version. Mother Goose as well as the classic fairy tales and Greek mythology all provide rich source material for endless spoofs or adaptations.

CREATING SIMPLE PUPPETS

PLACE ON FOLD

BASIC FABRIC BODY PATTERN

Basic Materials and Resource Bin

Standard materials needed to make the puppets shown in this book include basic items found in most schools. Keep the following items on hand:

—scissors
—white liquid glue
—a variety of colored construction paper
—stapler and staples
—Scotch tape and masking tape
—coloring tools such as crayon, felt-tip pens, and tempera paint

Resource Bin

A resource bin, filled with a variety of odds and ends, will enrich any puppet-making session as well as recycle throw-away items. Ask the students to bring in bags filled with scrap items: this, in itself, will constitute a valuable lesson in that it places value on items normally taken for granted. I have found children are often excited about showing off their "hand-collected" junk to others and that, in fact, they develop a sense of proprietorship toward these things.

A resource bin might include:

—food boxes of various sizes, such as spaghetti, oatmeal, jello, cake mixes, and detergent boxes
—egg cartons (plastic or cardboard)
—paper-towel or bathroom-tissue dowels
—plastic "bubbles" from packaged items
—styrofoam packing shapes, such as those found in appliance and shipping boxes
—aluminum foil and plastic food wrap
—paper plates, cups, drinking straws and ice cream sticks
—scrap fabric, yarns, buttons and trims
—old wallpaper and rug samples (available at trade stores)
—string, rubber bands and paper fastener brads
—dowels or sticks

Waxy surfaces

When securing items to a plastic or waxy surface you may need Scotch or masking tape. White glue does not adhere well to these surfaces, and therefore a substitute glue may be needed from a hardware or craft store. When painting waxy surfaces, add a small amount of liquid dishwashing detergent or "Future" floorwax to the paint to make it stick better. I recommend using latex wall paint (available at paint stores) and, in fact, I use it for all my puppets. Latex paint comes in bright colors and has a thicker, more adhesive base than tempera paint. Because it covers surfaces more easily, it is often less expensive to use than standard tempera paint. By purchasing quart-cans of red, blue, yellow, black and white you are then able to mix many colors in jars to keep on hand.

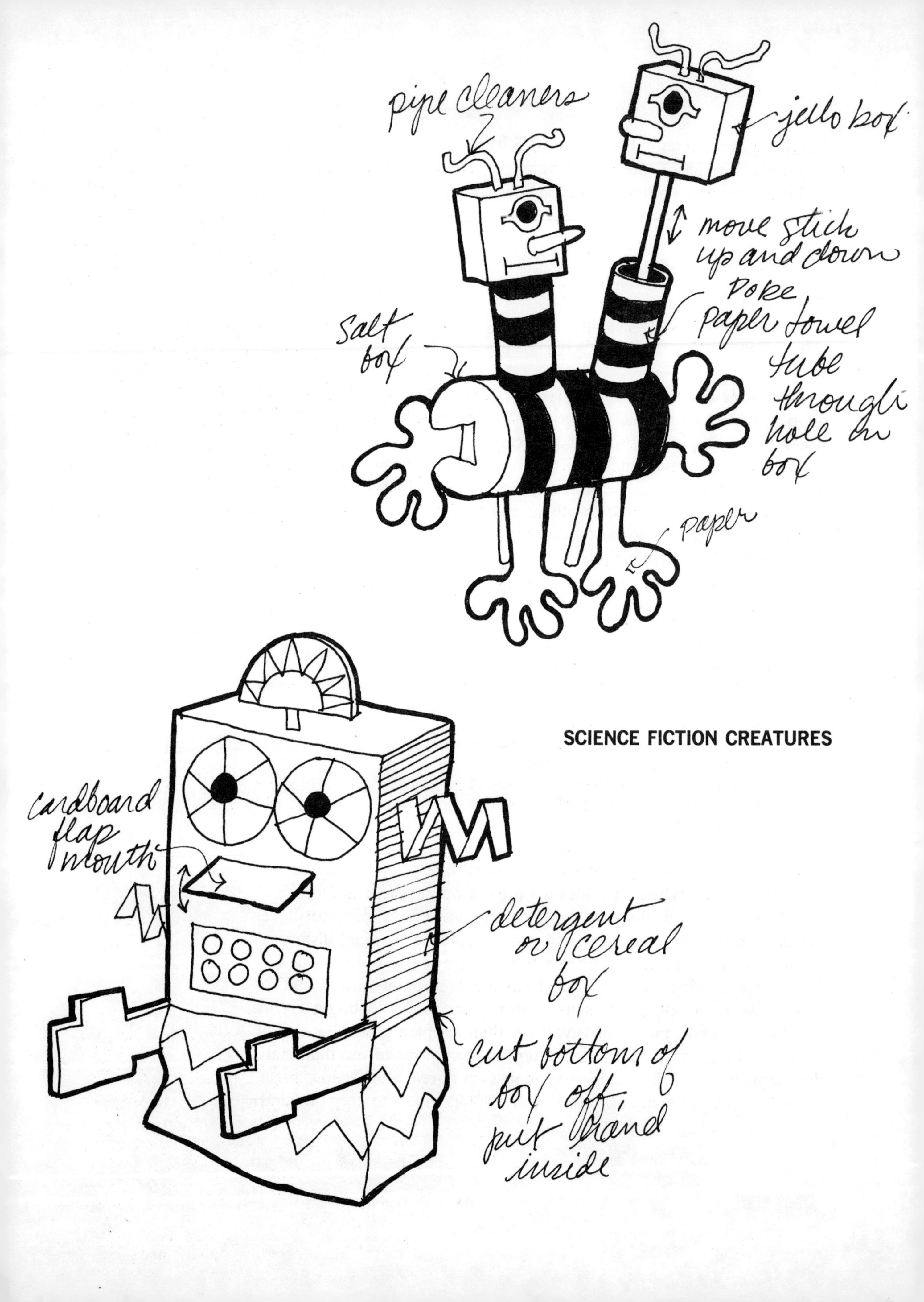
pipe cleaners
jello box
move stick up and down
poke paper towel tube through hole in box
salt box
paper
SCIENCE FICTION CREATURES
cardboard flap mouth
detergent or cereal box
cut bottom of box off put hand inside

Box Puppets

Boxes are beautiful! Because boxes are generally sturdy and come in infinite sizes and proportions, they are ideal structures for gluing and decorating.

Note: For boxes with waxy, paint-resistant surfaces, mix a small amount of liquid dish-washing detergent or Future floor wax with tempera paint so that it will adhere smoothly.

cardboard flap mouth; attach rubber band to underside of flap and insert finger to operate; move up and down
cut hole for finger
staple rubber band
fabric body

PANDA BEAR

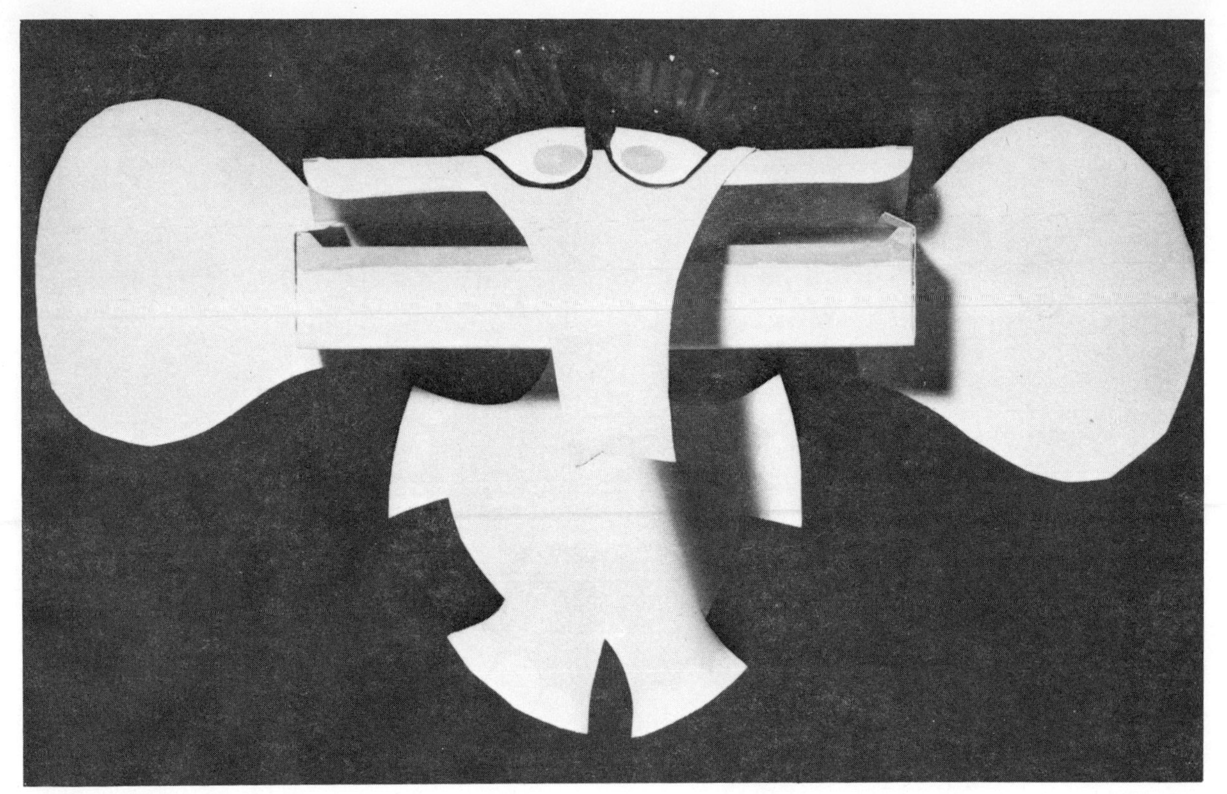

WAX-PAPER BOX—Elephant

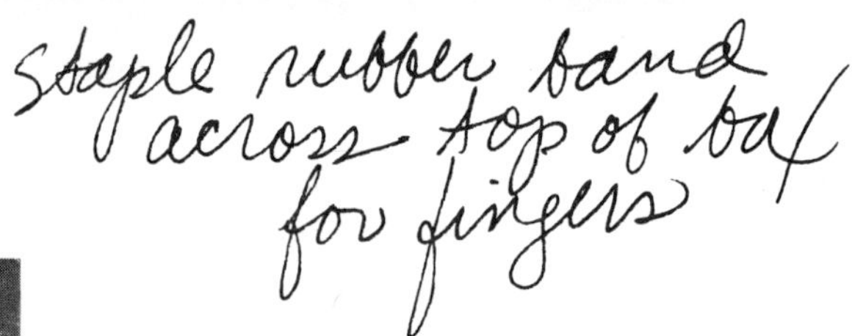

Staple rubber band across top of box for fingers

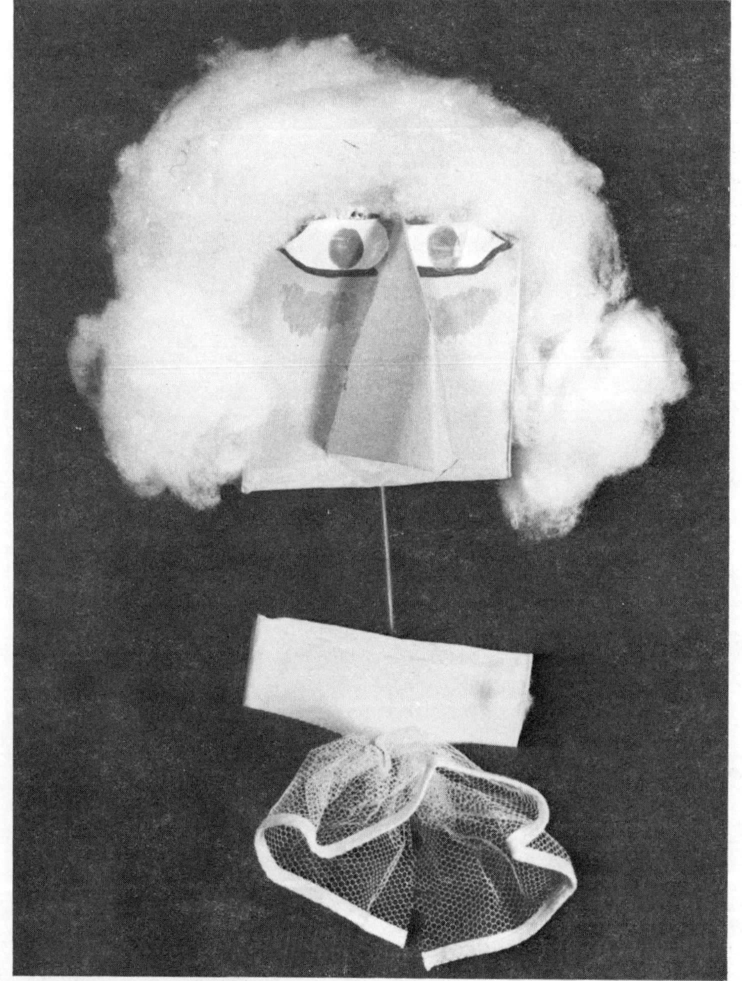

Cereal box - split in half; stick moves up and down for talking mouth

GEORGE WASHINGTON

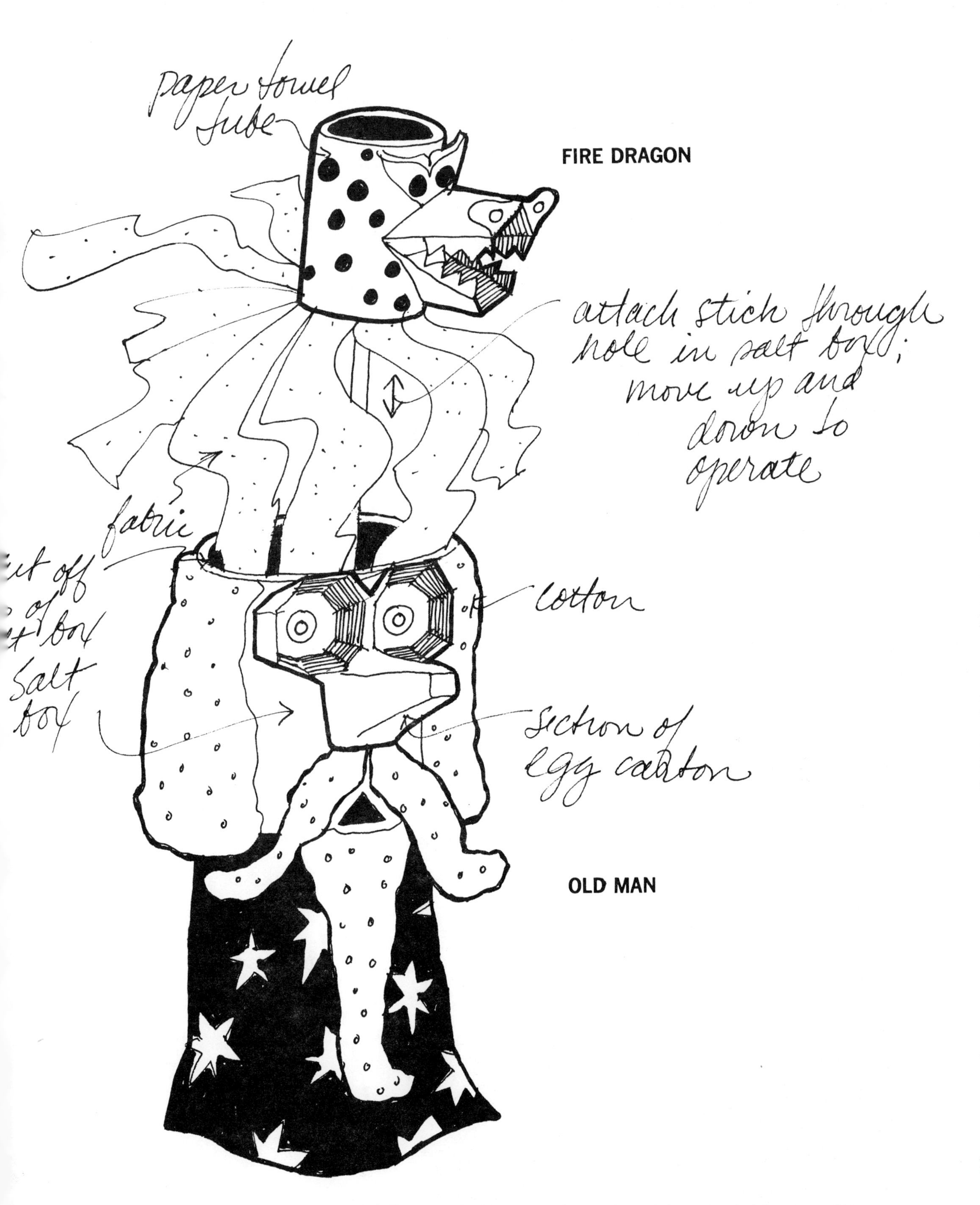

Puppet by Romelle Parker, Librarian, adapted from book "Everyone Knows What a Dragon Looks Like"—Jay Williams

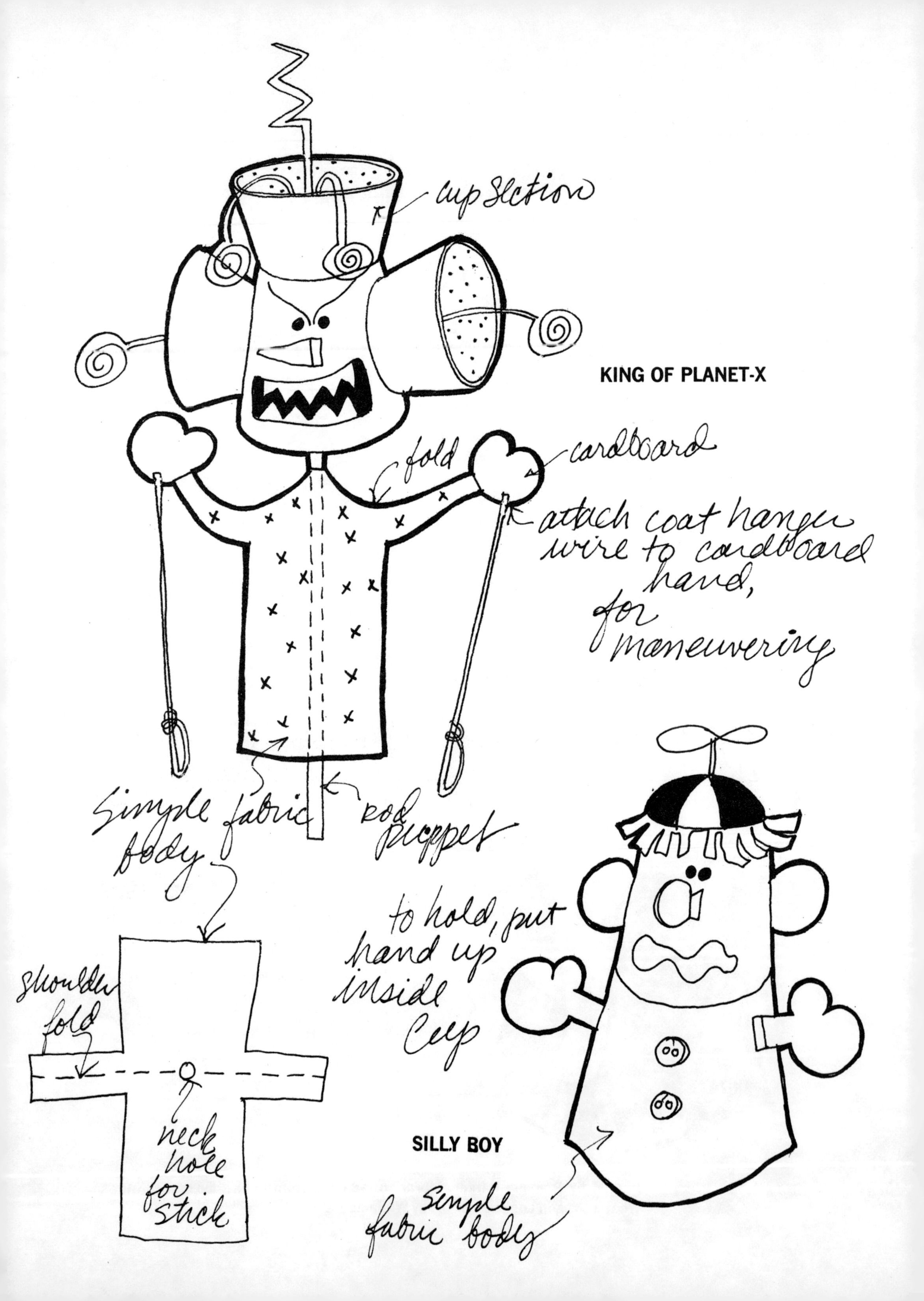
cup section
KING OF PLANET-X
fold
cardboard
attach coat hanger wire to cardboard hand, for maneuvering
Simple fabric body
rod puppet
shoulder fold
neck hole for stick
to hold, put hand up inside cup
SILLY BOY
Simple fabric body

Paper-Cup Puppets

Paper cups come in a variety of shapes and sizes—and so do puppets! Search the stores for various shapes, such as cone cups, mini-cups, styrofoam cups, or cups with handles, and add these to your resource collection for puppet-making. Children enjoy combining and stacking cups in different ways to create characters, and they also find them useful for building features onto other puppets.

INDIAN
move stick
up and down
to make
puppet
talk
PIRATE

cup
hold handles of cups with two hands to operate
paper towel tube
one-piece fabric body hangs over paper towel tube shoulders
Excellent puppet for table-top performances (see page 129)

MAYOR

Paper-Plate Puppets

One of the most versatile materials for puppet-making is the paper plate. Both in texture and shape, it is a material with seemingly endless possibilities. It is made from paper stock flexible enough to be bent and curved but strong enough to have substance as it is painted and glued. Its basic shape, the perfect circle, is conducive to many animal and human forms and can also be cut into other shapes which happily combine into faces and features at the imagination's will.

Collect a varied stock of paper plates for puppet-making; keep plenty of round plates, for example, in both small and large sizes. Try to obtain special paper plates such as hot-dog, soup-bowl, and oval plates to diversify the puppets. For added interest, collect a variety of paper cups (standard, miniature, cone-shaped, etc.), drinking straws, egg cartons, and paper-towel tubes to enrich any puppet-making project.

Constructing the Puppets

A durable, basic paper-plate hand puppet can be constructed by stapling two paper plates together around the outer edges, then inserting and gluing a paper-towel tube between them. Cut and sew a fabric body (as shown on page 68) and glue it to the tube neck.

try cutting away a plate to create a "profile" with funny noses

2 paper plates
glue paper towel tube between plates

basic fabric body

ANT-MAN
GIRAFFE
try combining plates
long tube
BOY

Paper-Plate Talking Mouth Puppets

Young children, particularly, enjoy these special "loud-mouth" puppets which open wide to expose tonsils, teeth, and tongues. They are invaluable in encouraging speech (particularly loud speech) and dialogue, and have also been used successfully in conjunction with dental and health care lessons. In general these puppets are better made from large paper plates, but smaller plates might be appropriate for certain characters, such as a talking apple, a wailing baby, or a chattering chipmunk.

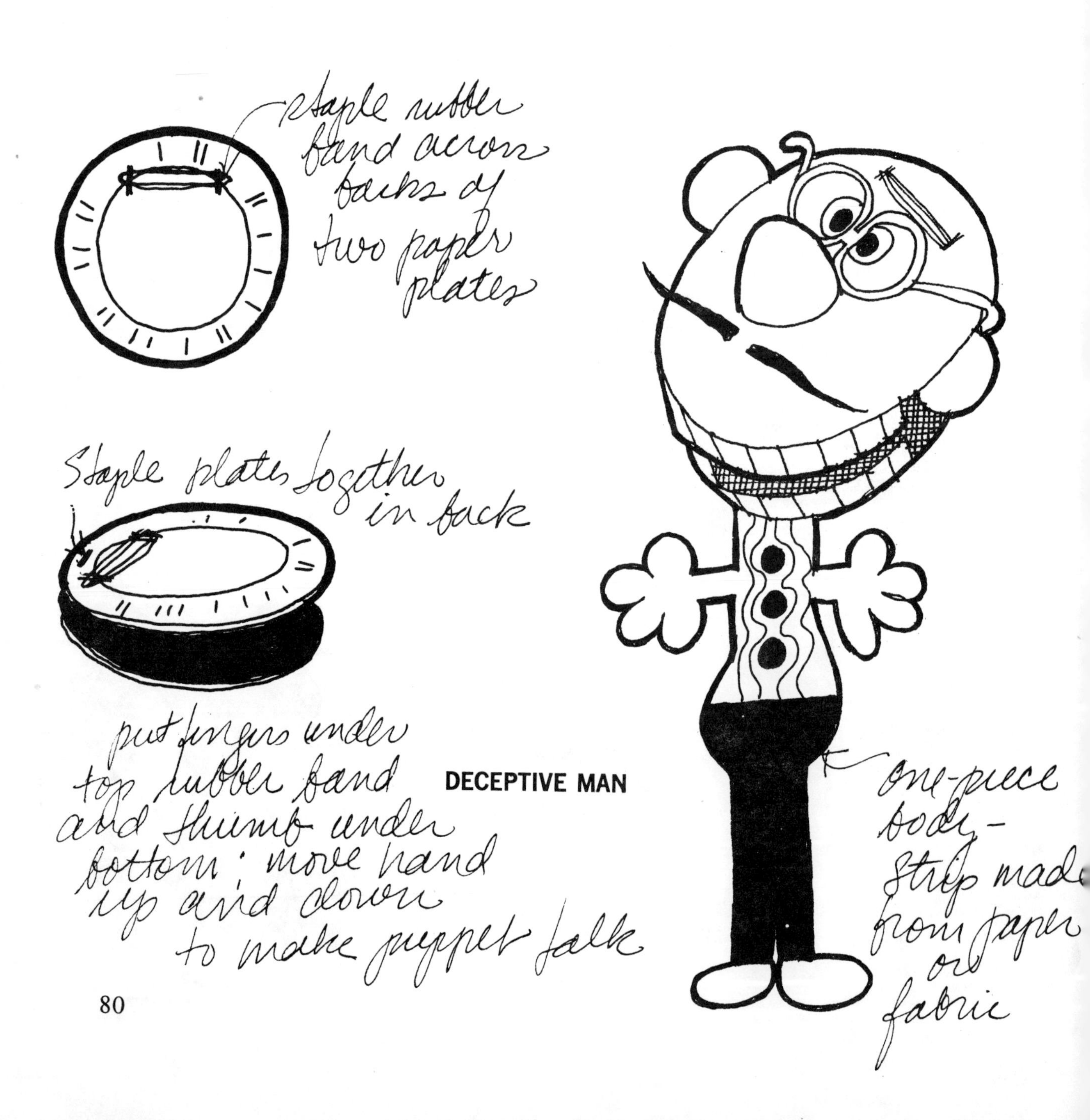
staple rubber band across backs of two paper plates
Staple plates together in back
put fingers under top rubber band and thumb under bottom; move hand up and down to make puppet talk
DECEPTIVE MAN
one-piece body-strip made from paper or fabric

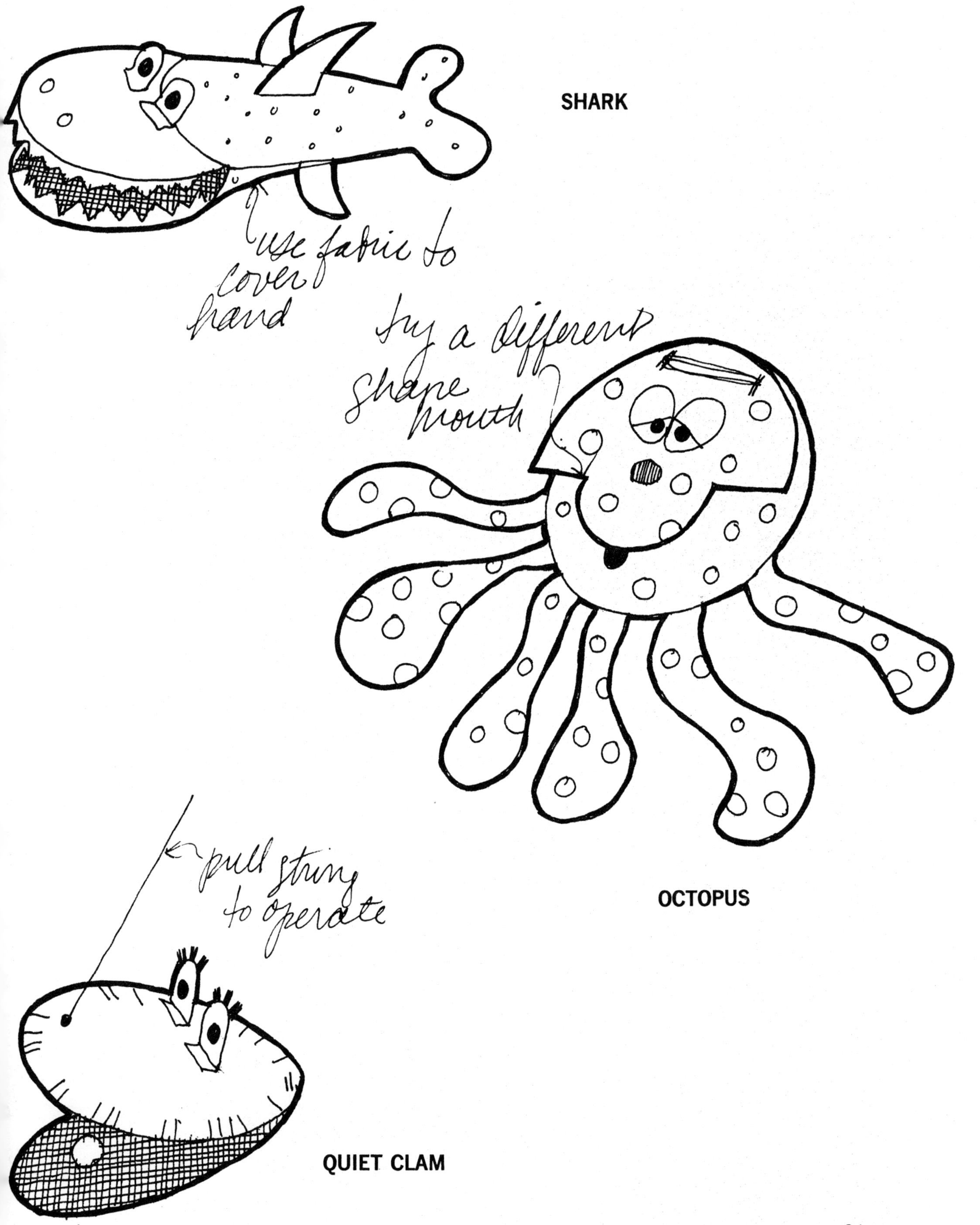
SHARK
use fabric to cover hand
try a different shape mouth
OCTOPUS
pull string to operate
QUIET CLAM

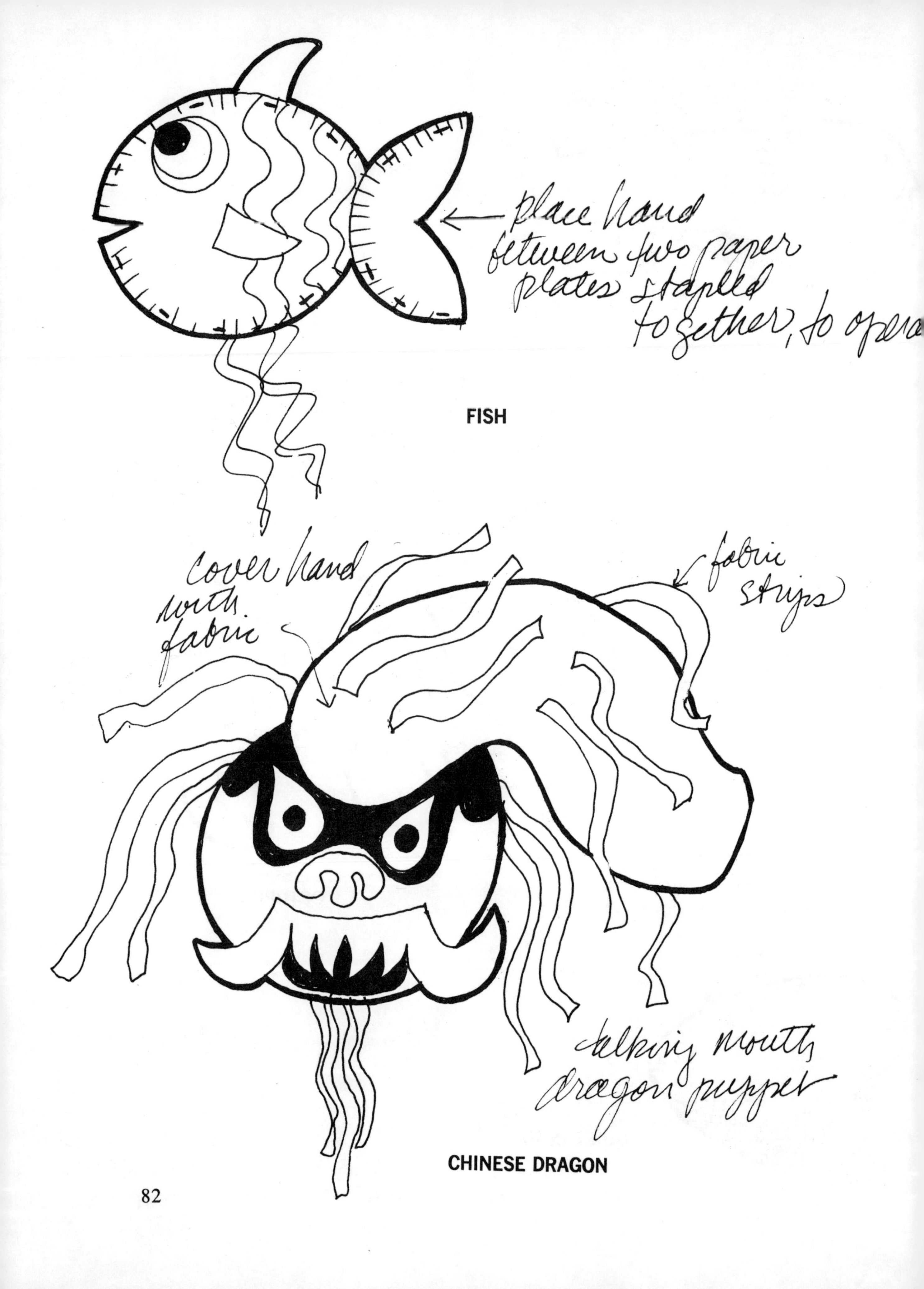
place hand
between two paper
plates stapled
together, to opera
cover hand
with
fabric
fabric
strips
talking mouth
dragon puppet

FISH

CHINESE DRAGON

Exploring the Paper Plate

Using your supply of large and small paper plates, feel completely free to cut any shapes and to experiment with combinations of these dissected shapes. Paper-fastener brads aid in creating puppets with movable parts. As different puppet forms emerge, decide upon the best method of operating the new creation, whether it be string, rod or simple hand control.

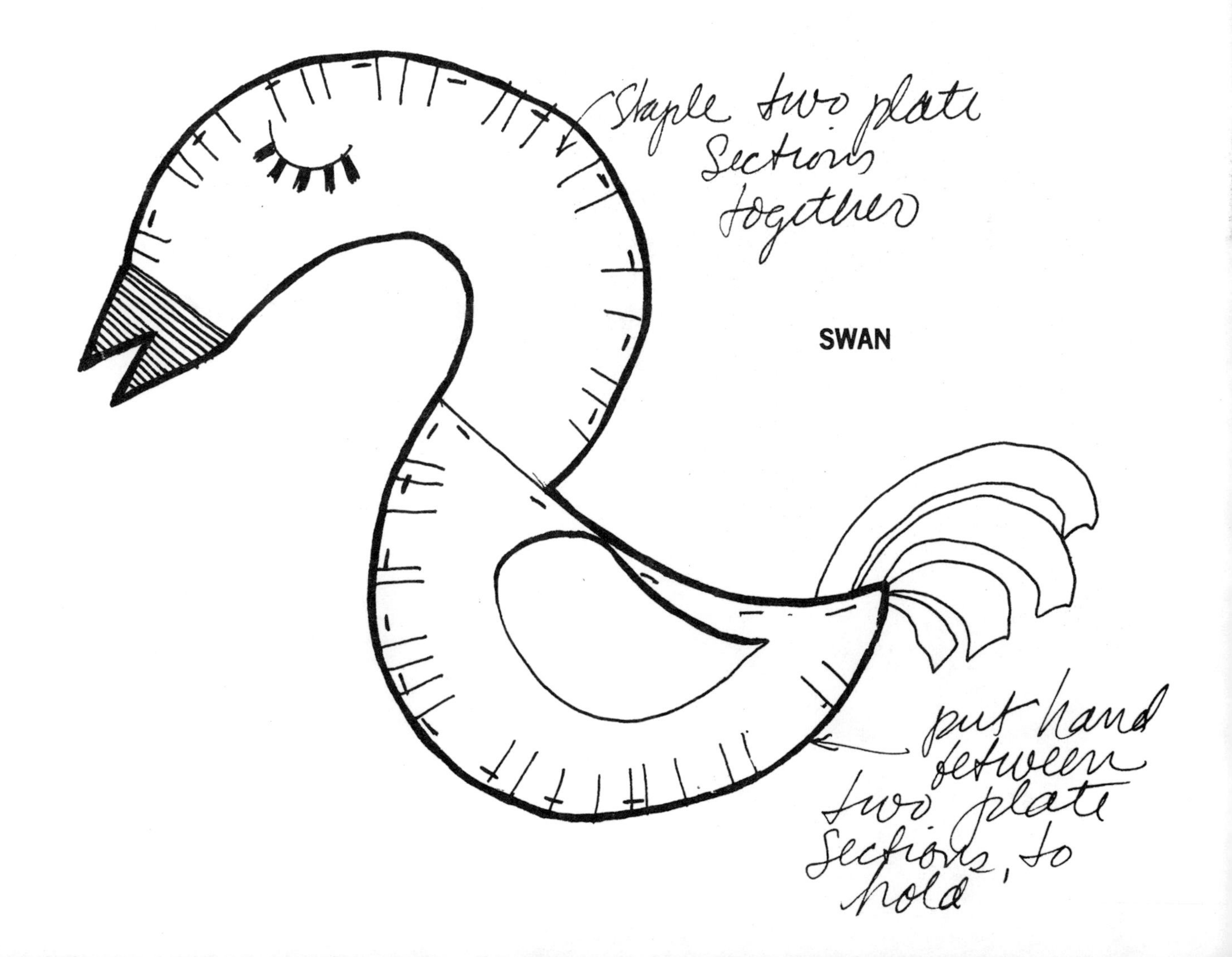
Staple two plate Sections together
SWAN
put hand between two plate Sections, to hold

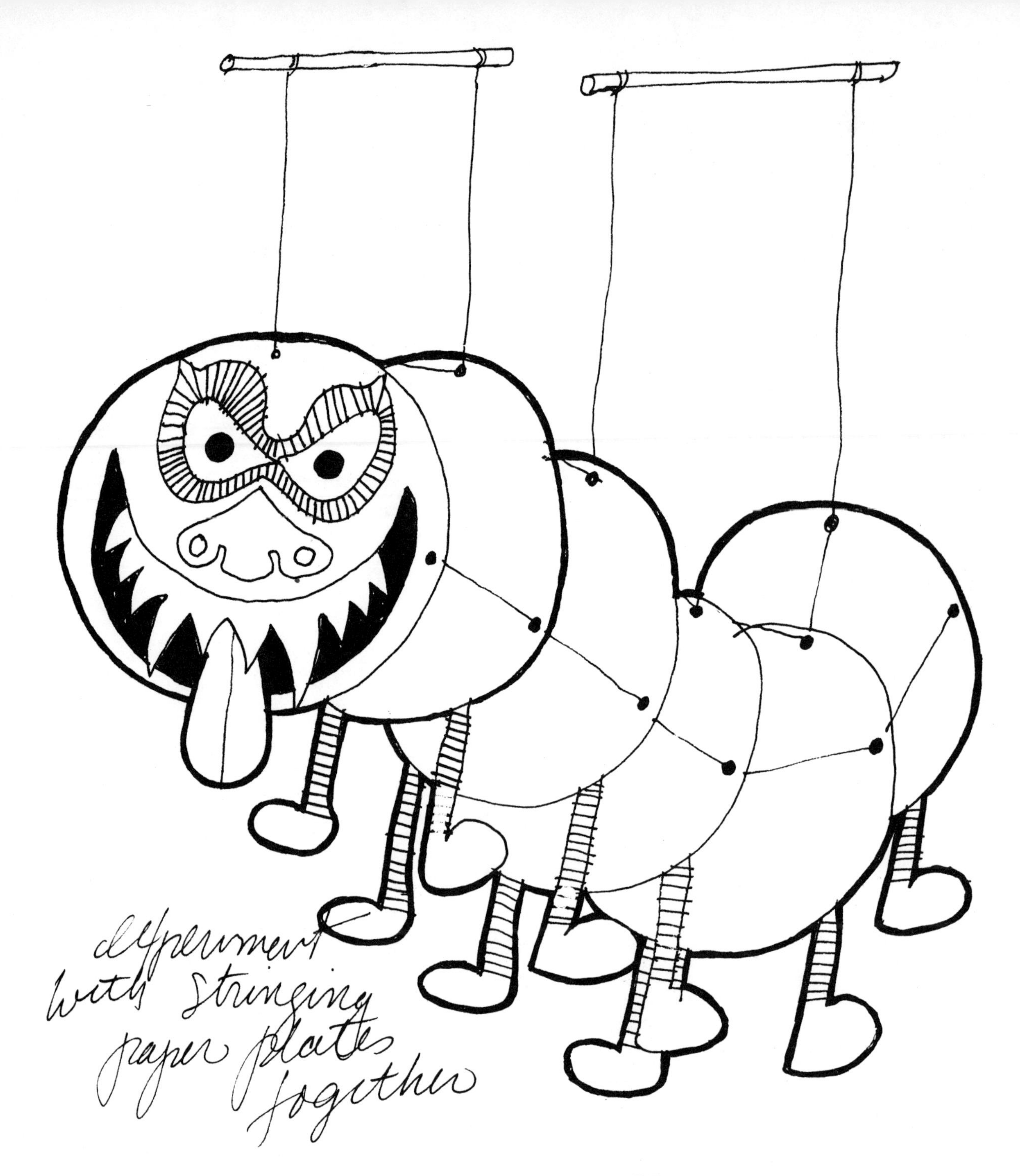
experiment
with stringing
paper plates
together

DRAGON

Stuffed-Paper-Bag Puppets

There is nothing quite so humble as the brown paper bag, nor is there anything as readily available, durable and diverse for puppet-making. Designed specifically to be durable, paper bags are excellent for painting and gluing. It is fun to explore the various sizes and shapes with which paper bags abound, especially the extremities such as a giant grocery bag puppet or the thin, long umbrella or bottle bag puppet .

Stuffed paper bag puppets are excellent for older students, who desire a more professional end product. When properly completed, these puppets are comparable in quality to the more complicated paper mache puppets but considerably less laborious to make. They also have the added versatility of being hand, rod, or string operated.

Hand or Rod Stuffed-Paper-Bag Puppets

Tightly stuff a small-medium, study paper bag with wadded, crumpled up newspaper. Insert and glue a paper-towel tube into the neck of the bag. Tightly gather the opening and wrap it with masking tape to secure it in place. Cut and sew a fabric body as shown on page 68 . Glue it to the tube neck for a hand type puppet; or glue and insert a stick inside bag for a rod-controlled puppet.

OUTER-SPACE PILOT

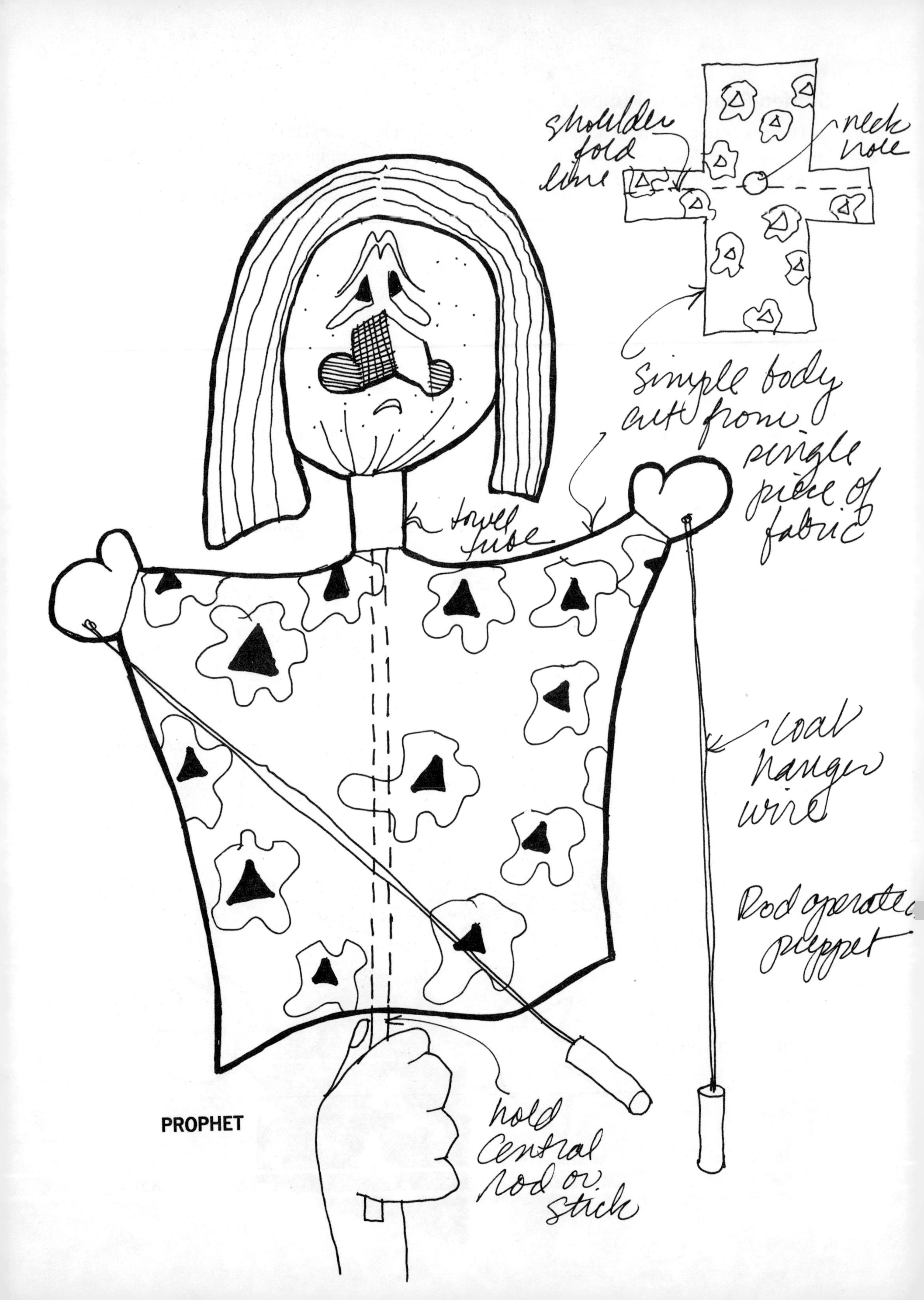
shoulder fold line
neck hole
simple body cut from single piece of fabric
towel tube
coat hanger wire
Rod operated puppet
hold central rod or stick

PROPHET

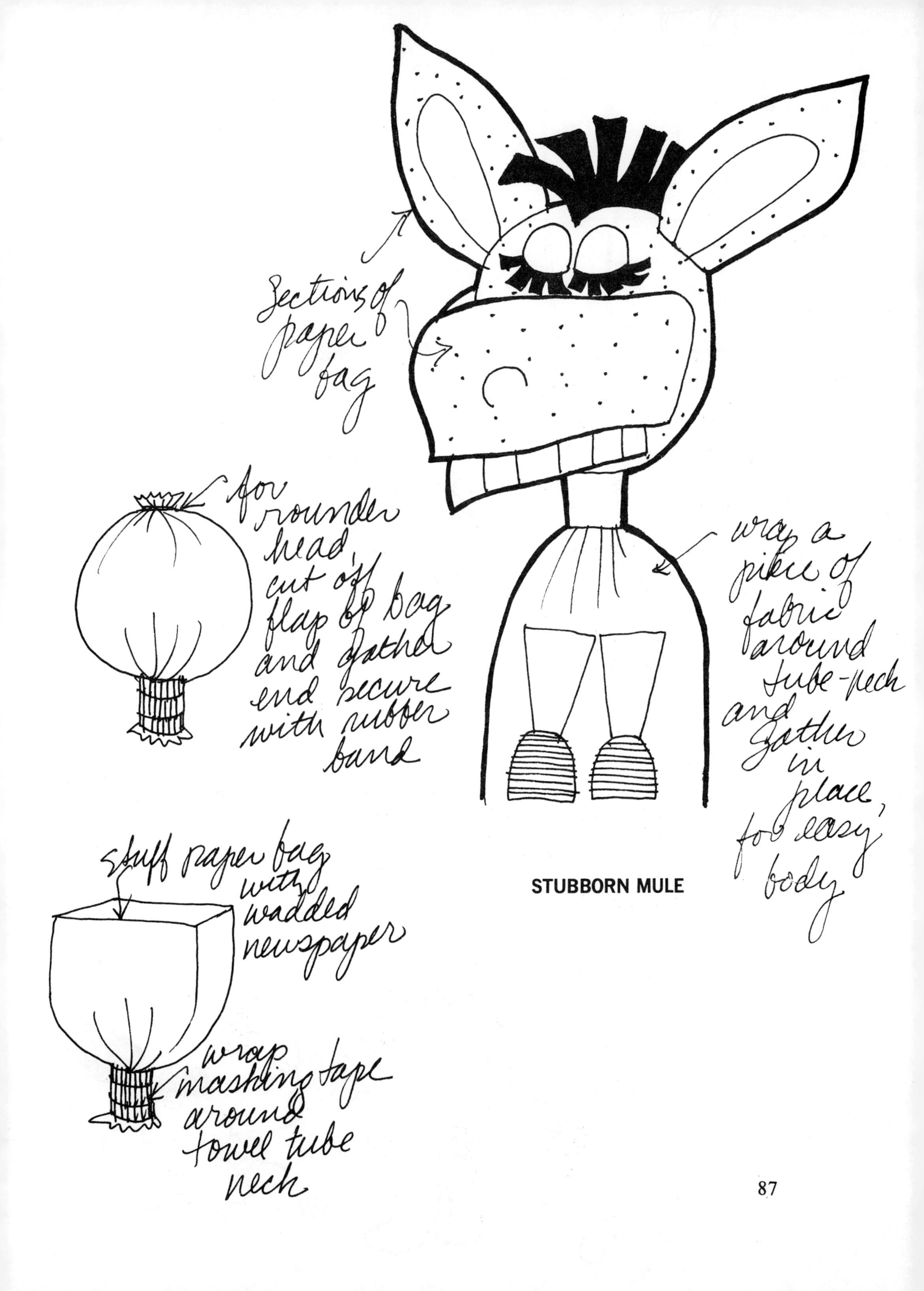
Sections of paper bag
for rounder head, cut off flap of bag and gather end secure with rubber band
wrap a piece of fabric around tube-neck and gather in place, for easy body
stuff paper bag with wadded newspaper
wrap masking tape around towel tube neck

STUBBORN MULE

BIRD

HOUNDDOG

Stuffed-Paper-Bag String Puppets

Older students are thoroughly intrigued by the mechanical aspects of a string-operated puppet or marionette and take pride in their mechanical prowess in developing such a puppet. But while marionettes or string puppets are fun to create and to use, they are limited in their ability to be manipulated. Since these puppets do not move as freely as hand-operated ones, they are less suited to younger children, who best express themselves on a spontaneous level.

Even the simplest of marionettes can do more than simply "bounce" about on strings. It is important to give children extra time to practice movement with their puppets, before a mirror, if possible. They should work on subtleties such as walking, running, waving good-bye, and nodding the head.

In storing these puppets, be careful to avoid tangling the strings. Professionals often hold the strings of one puppet together and deliberately spin the puppet around until the strings are "twisted" together. When the puppet is ready to be used, it is simply unwound in reverse to free the strings.

Constructing the Puppets

An assortment of creatures may be made by combining a variety of stuffed bags. It is easiest to lay the unstuffed bags onto a table and link them together, as shown, with string prior to stuffing. Use a sturdy flexible string, such as nylon fishing line or other hardware string; avoid weak strings, such as yarn, sewing thread, or kite string.

A marionette is at the complete mercy of the few strings that operate its limited motions; accordingly, one must give particular thought to just which parts of the puppet should be movable.

Limbs made from rolled newspapers can be used in conjunction with bags. Roll up two or three sheets of folded newspaper into a very tight "jellyroll" with a supporting string positioned in the center. Then attach the strings at the joints or to the hands and feet. Weight the hands and feet to achieve nimble movement, by adding pieces of clay or taping washers, bolts, or other metal weights to the ends. You are then ready to construct a costume over this basic "newspaper skeleton."

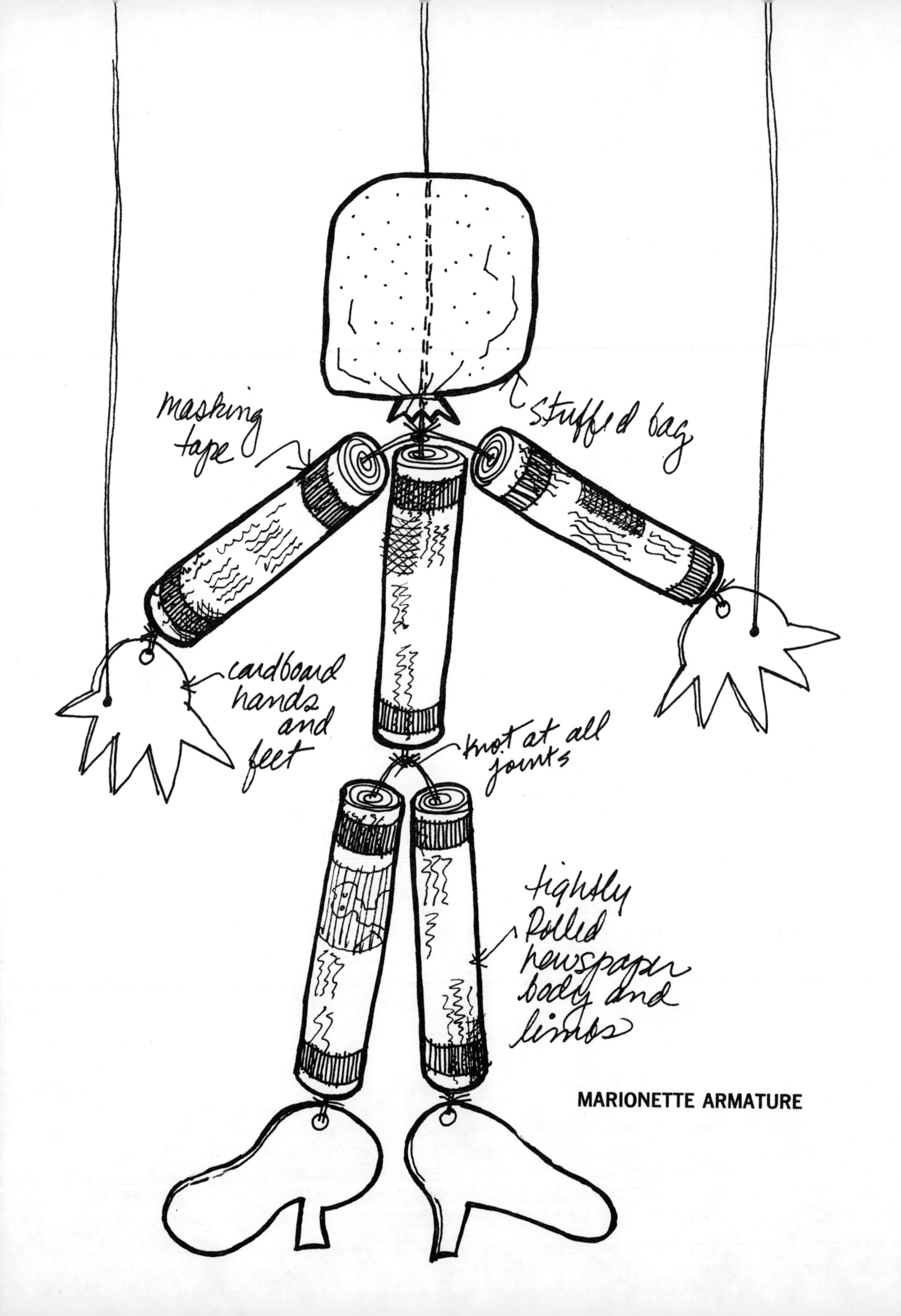

MARIONETTE ARMATURE

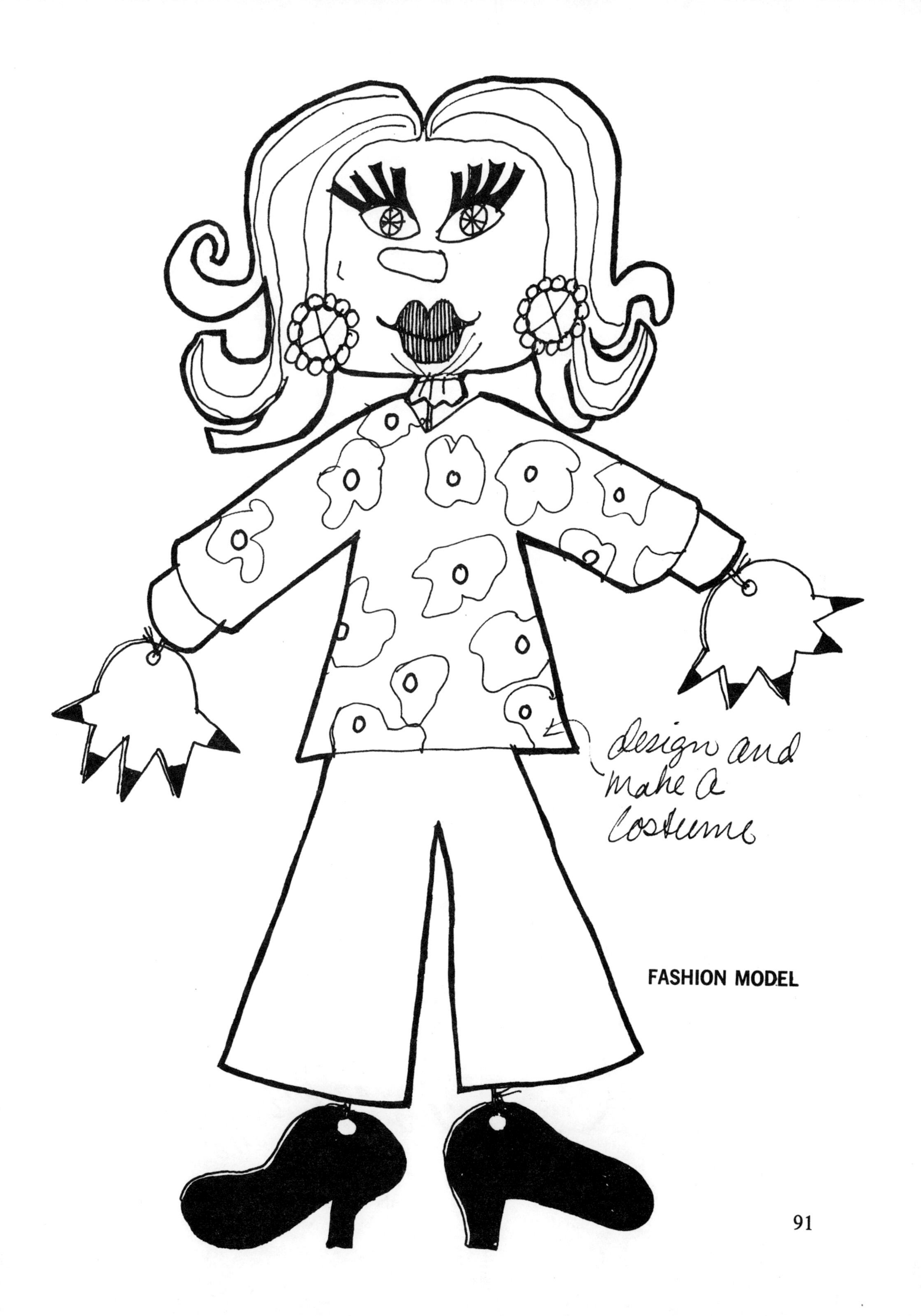
design and
make a
costume

FASHION MODEL

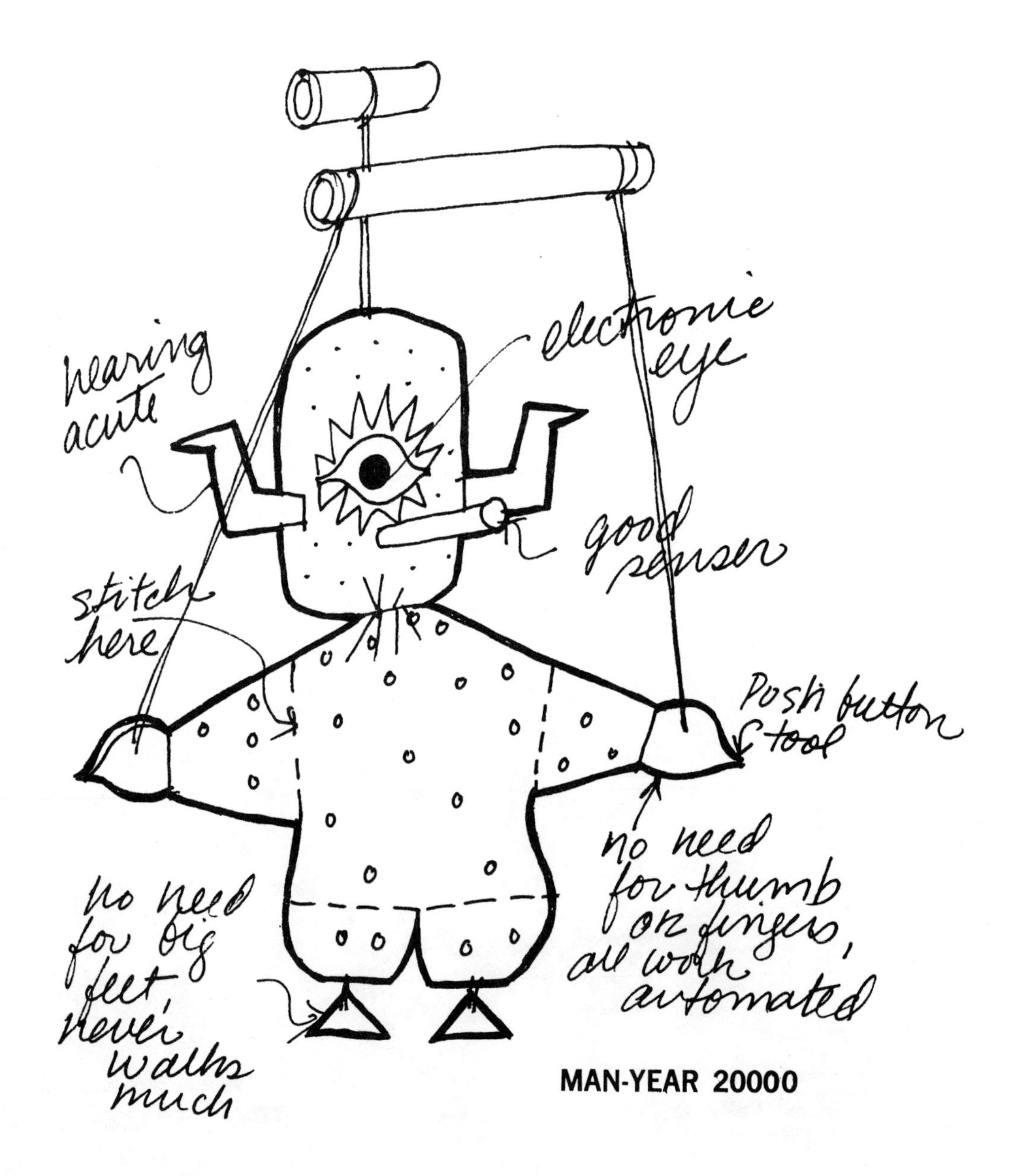

MAN-YEAR 20000

Stuffed-Paper-Bag String Puppets with Fabric Body

Children who enjoy sewing can make more advanced string puppets by using a stuffed paper bag for the head and creating a body from fabric.

Constructing the Puppets

First have the student design a body pattern from a sheet of folded newspaper by drawing half a body shape with a crayon or felt-tip marker; cut out the body shape and open up the newspaper to reveal a complete body. If the body appears too large or too small experiment with alternate designs. Pin the newspaper pattern to fabric and cut out two duplicate pieces, a front and a back. Pin or baste the right sides of the front and back pieces together and sew around the edges as shown, leaving neck, hands, and feet areas open. Turn the body right side out through the neck opening; sew and stuff the body areas as shown. *Do not stuff the arms and legs*; these should be loose for mobility. Glue the neck of the fabric body to the stuffed paper-bag neck. Cardboard hands and feet may also be attached to the body. Experiment with weighting the hands and feet, if necessary, by adding plastic-clay or taping on metal items such as washers and bolts.

Paper-mache heads made over clay or balloon forms may also be used with this type of puppet.

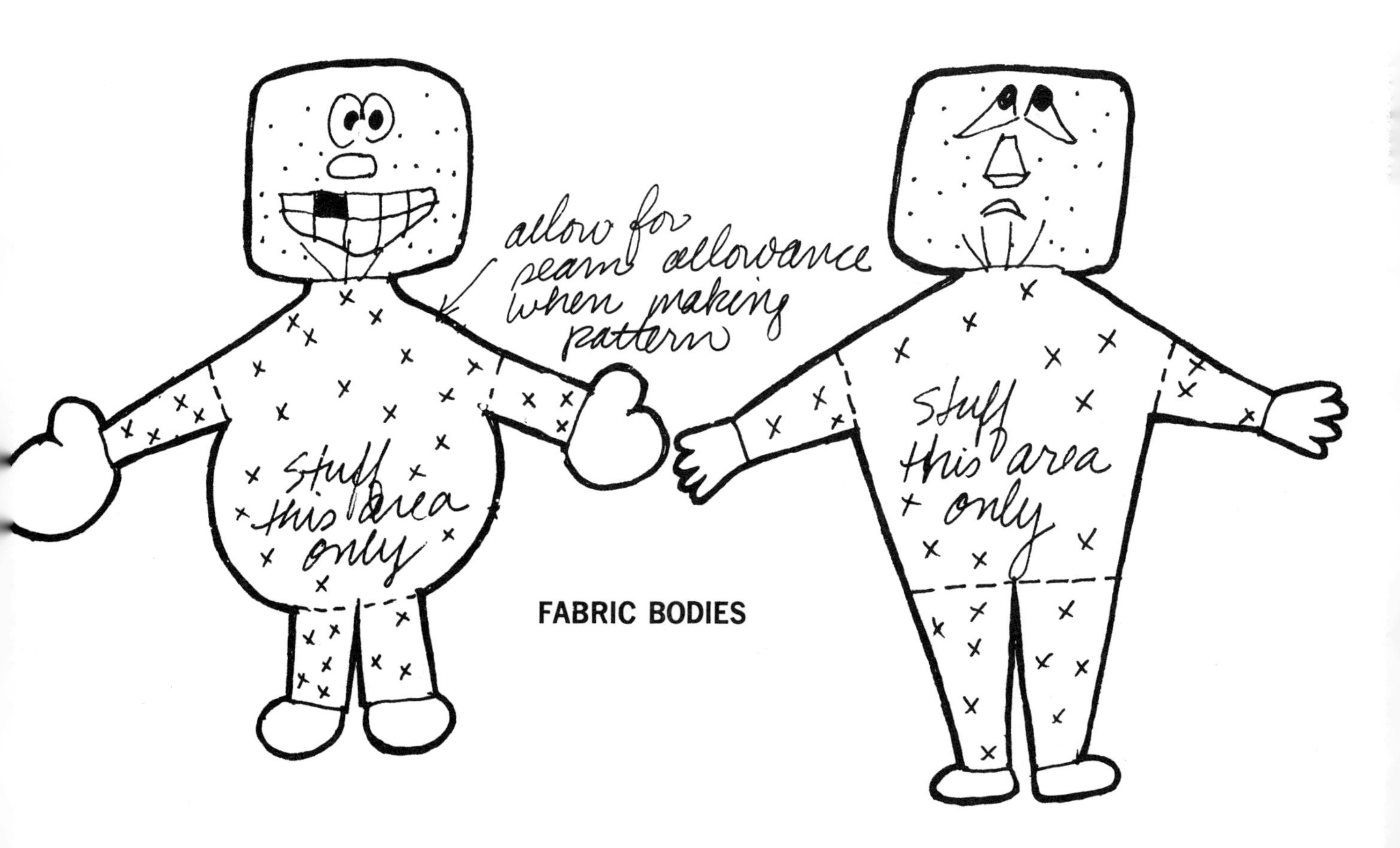

FABRIC BODIES

Stuffed-Paper-Rod Puppets

Large bold shapes cut out of sturdy paper, such as grocery bags or mural paper, offer endless possibilities for creating puppet characters. Once painted, textured or otherwise decorated, these puppets are placed upon rods and become bold, highly mobile puppets.

Constructing the Puppets

To make a stuffed-paper-rod puppet, first draw and cut out two identical shapes which will represent the puppet character. Staple or glue the two shapes together three-quarters of the way around the entire edge, being careful to leave an opening to place the stuffing. Now fill the shape with crumpled newspaper until it is as full as you wish. Staple the remaining edge, leaving a small bottom opening through which you can insert a wooden stick or rod. Glue this handle in place.

Operating the Puppets

To operate the puppet, hold the rod and manipulate the puppet from below. It may be moved above a stage opening or simply out in the open space of a room.

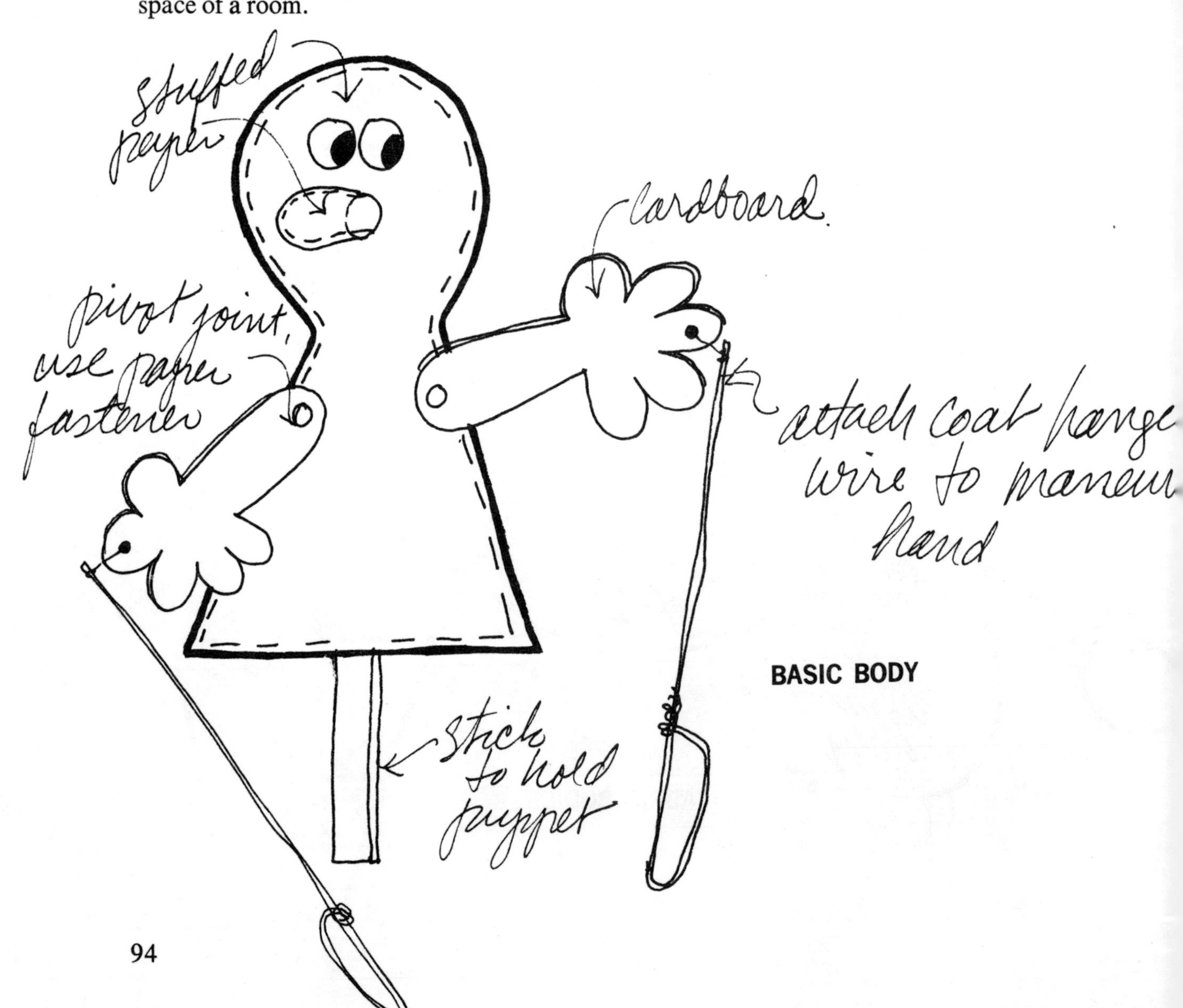

BASIC BODY

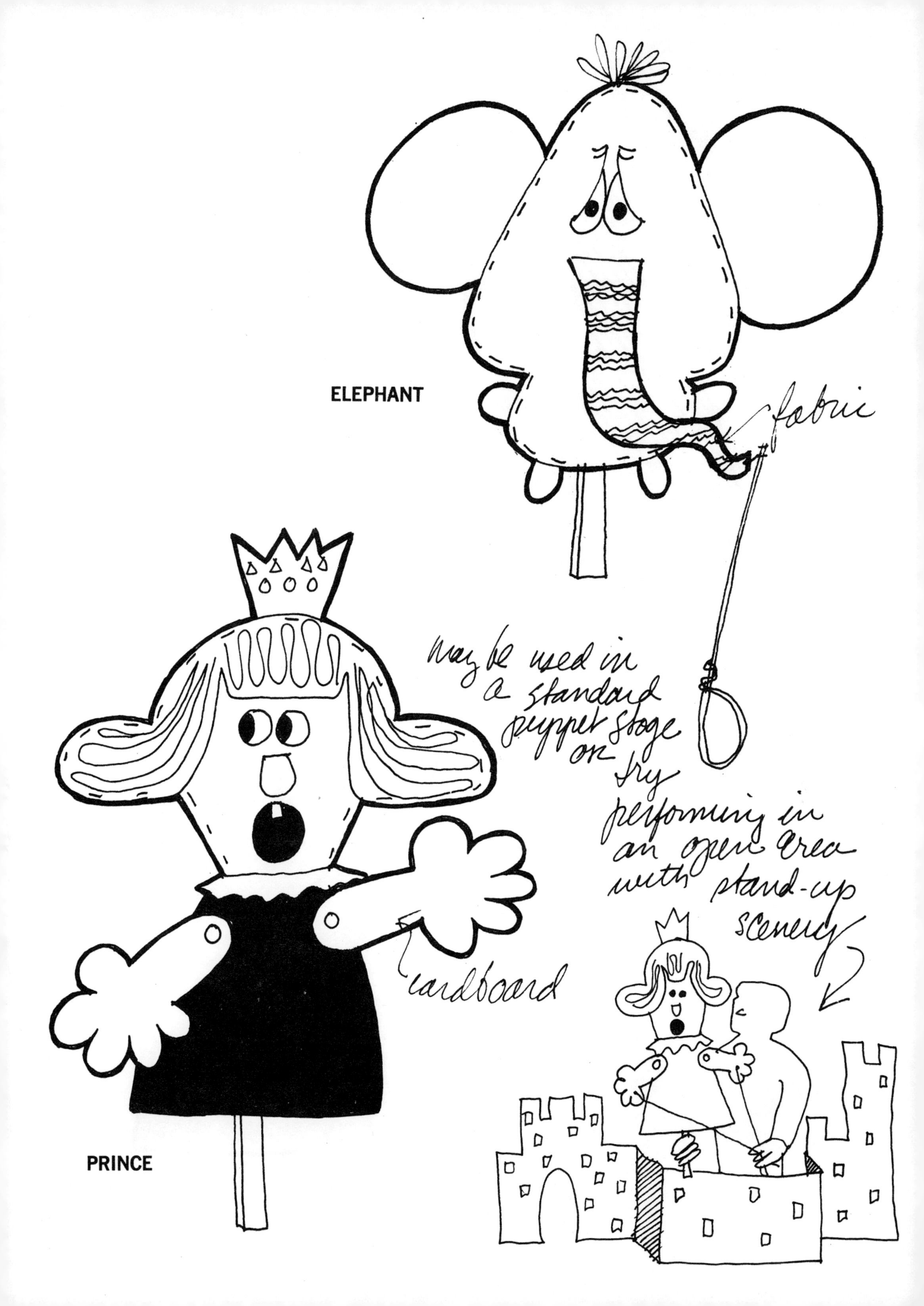
ELEPHANT
fabric
may be used in a standard puppet stage or try performing in an open area with stand-up scenery
cardboard
PRINCE

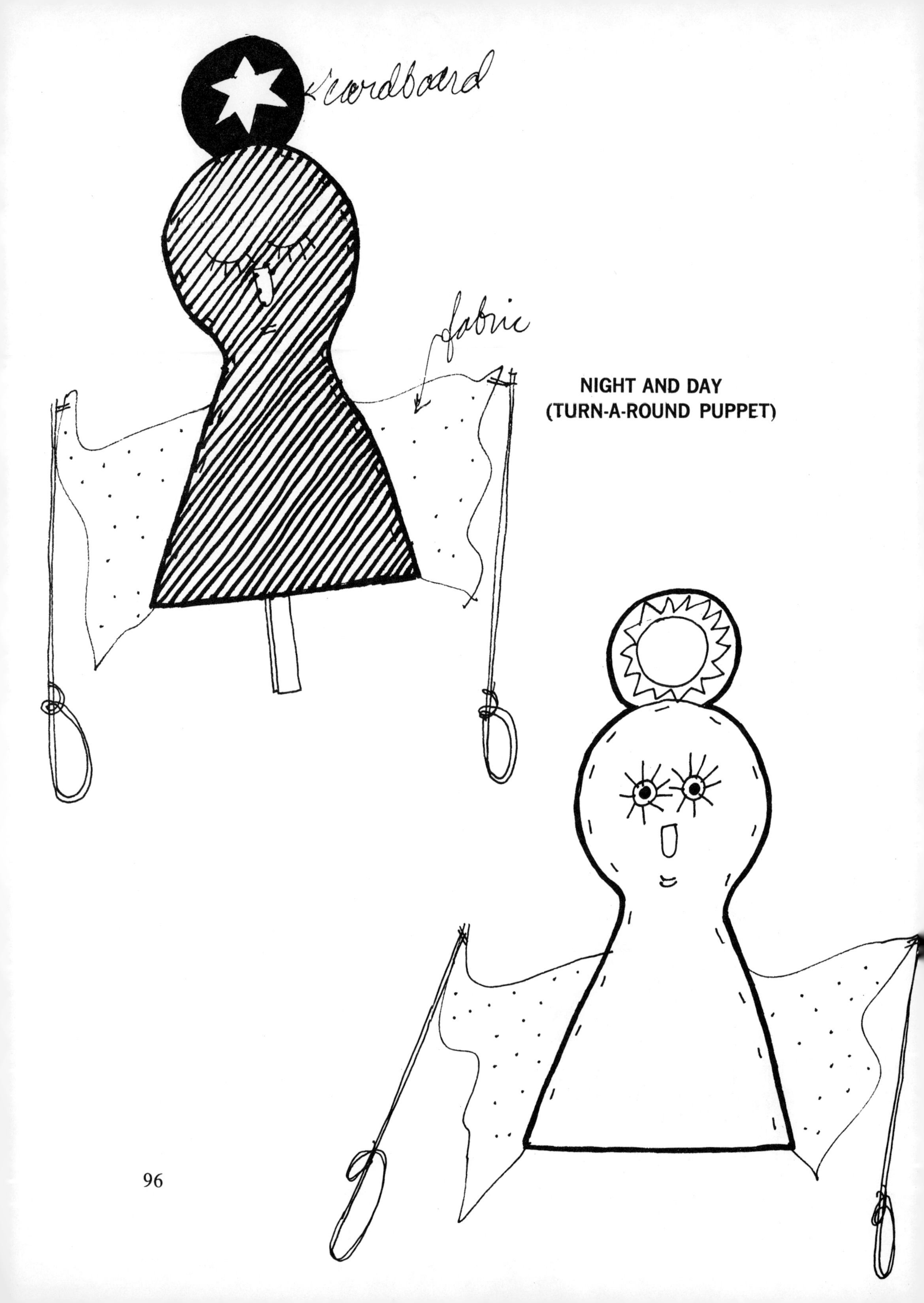

NIGHT AND DAY
(TURN-A-ROUND PUPPET)

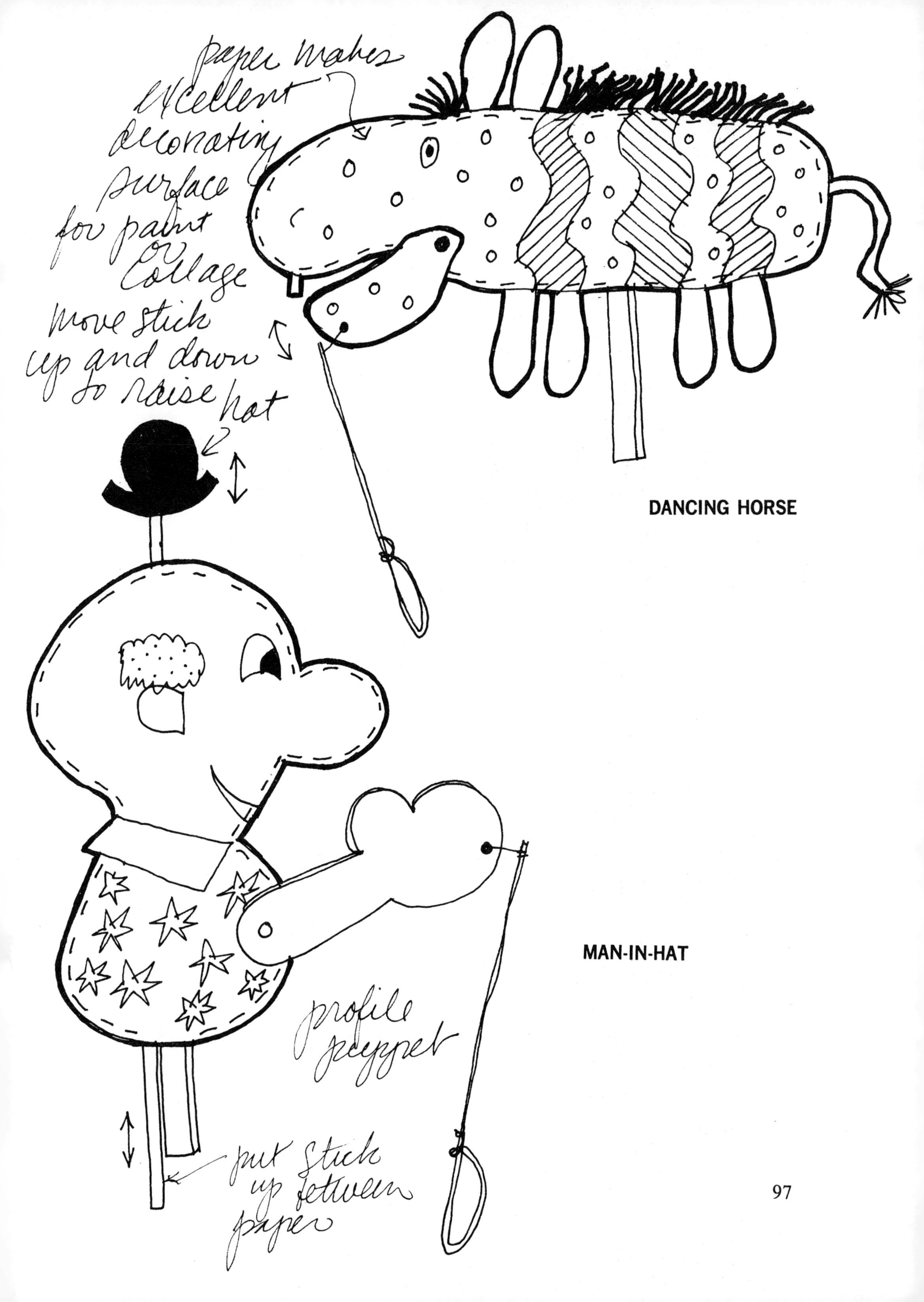

paper makes excellent decorating surface for paint or collage
move stick up and down to raise hat
profile puppet
put stick up between paper

DANCING HORSE

MAN-IN-HAT

stuff sock
with
soft
material
wrap
masking
tape around
towel tube
neck

NY

BASEBALL PLAYER

GOAT

Stuffed-Sock Puppets

Search out varied textured and patterned socks that lend themselves well to puppet creations. Almost any sock has potential for a puppet, but particularly adaptable are stretch socks (especially those without heels).

Constructing the Puppets

To make a standard puppet head, cut off a length of man's or woman's sock seven to eight inches from the end of the toe. Use polyester fiber fill, shredded scrap fabric, or soft paper toweling to stuff and shape the sock as desired; you way want additional stuffing in certain areas, such as cheeks and forehead. Insert a paper towel tube into the stuffing and glue it at the neck, gathering the sock opening closed. Wrap masking tape around the gathered neck opening until it is secure.

Other parts of the sock may be used to create a nose, snout, or ears. These, too, can be stuffed and attached to the basic head. Scraps of felt also make excellent features.

Cut and sew a fabric body (as shown on page 68) and glue it to the towel tube.

GRANNY

Stuffed-Stocking Puppets

Using recycled stockings to create puppets produces results which resemble fantastic soft sculptures. Older students, particularly, are fascinated by this art form and have the skill necessary to master the hand-sewing which is an integral part of stuffed-stocking puppets. These puppets with their gnarled, human-like appearance often take on an uncanny realism.

Constructing the Puppets

To make a stuffed-stocking puppet, first cut off from the end of the toe a length of stocking approximately seven to eight inches; or from the leg section cut off an equal length, which has been sewn off at one end. Next loosen up polyester fiber fill by tearing it apart with the fingers. Fill the stocking section with these polyester pieces, gently pushing them around to mold a shape. Slip a paper-towel tube into the stuffing at neck opening, making sure it is well hidden. Wrap masking tape around the opening to secure the stocking to the tube.

To define the features of the puppet's face, you might puff out cheeks with the point of a needle or pinch in eves with the fingers. Use a felt-tip marker to indicate areas to be sewn. Be sure that the drawn areas are larger than you anticipate the finished feature to be, for it will "shrink" during sewing. Beginning and ending all sewing with an overcast stitch (because knots easily pull out), follow the outlines of the features with your needle to sew small running stitches along all lines. Pull the thread gently while simultaneously puckering out the sewn area with the needle point to further define and shape the features. If you wish a larger nose that stands out from the basic head, you may attach a fabric-stuffed nose of a matching color to the stocking face. For the finishing touches, use powdered cosmetics such as blusher and eye shadow to add color and make-up to the face, especially to define the lips and eye areas. You may also find colored felt-tip markers useful to further define facial features.

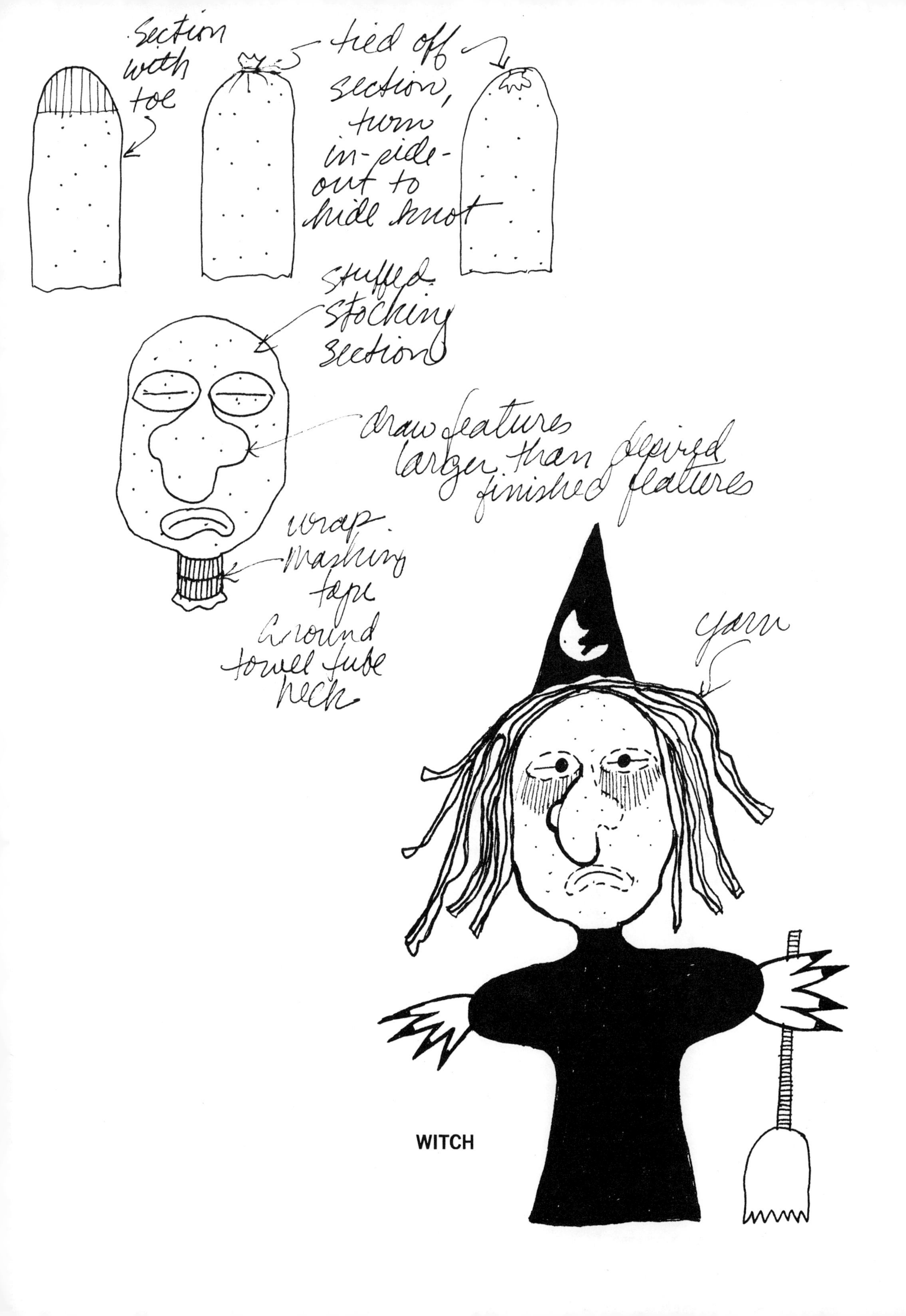
section with toe
tied off section, turn in-side-out to hide knot
stuffed stocking section
draw features larger than desired finished features
wrap masking tape around towel tube neck
yarn

WITCH

MOUSE **HAWAIIAN GIRL**

draw features with felt tip pen, follow lines with running stitches!

DOG
OLD LADY
felt or fabric ears
try a two-piece head
add a larger nose if desired

Overhead Shadow Puppets

Overhead shadow puppetry is an exciting and predominantly unexplored medium, which lends itself well to the classroom or library. Its basic use of the overhead projector makes it one of the few puppet forms belonging almost exclusively to the classroom or library. Furthermore, because only minimal effort is required to produce effective results, overhead shadow puppetry is an area deserving full attention and exploration.

Constructing the puppets

Cut out characters from oak tag, manila folders, or poster board. Use small pointed scissors to cut out detailed features, and a hole puncher to punch out eyes and also holes for joints with moving parts; secure the movable parts with paper fasteners. Animal tails, whiskers, hair and spider legs can be made with bits of yarn, string, or thread. Transparent fabric, lace or paper doilies, and other perforated materials further embellish these puppets when seen in shadow. Attach plastic straws to backs of puppets with pieces of masking tape for manipulating.

Operating the puppets

Place puppets on top of the projector and move them with the attached straw handles. Bend the straws slightly to prevent obstruction of the light source. To achieve distinctive characters, experiment by moving them in various ways. A cow could move very slowly, a goat might hop sprightly, and a bird might fly up and down.

Scenery

Scenery adds color and life to the skit. Use plastic sheets of acetate (which usually accompany projectors) as a medium upon which to create scenes with marking pens—a castle, a barnyard, etc. A "moving scene" can be created by Scotch taping together several sheets of acetate and moving them slowly, while manipulating the puppets on top.

Special Effects

Special effects add fun to shadow puppet productions. *HUMPTY DUMPTY* can "split" apart at the pre-cracked seam; the *I KNOW AN OLD LADY WHO SWALLOWED A FLY* can expand at the stomach by means of a piece of fabric added to the middle of her stomach; or *THE ELEPHANT'S CHILD* can actually appear to "grow" a long trunk by means of a strip of paper pulling away from the head.

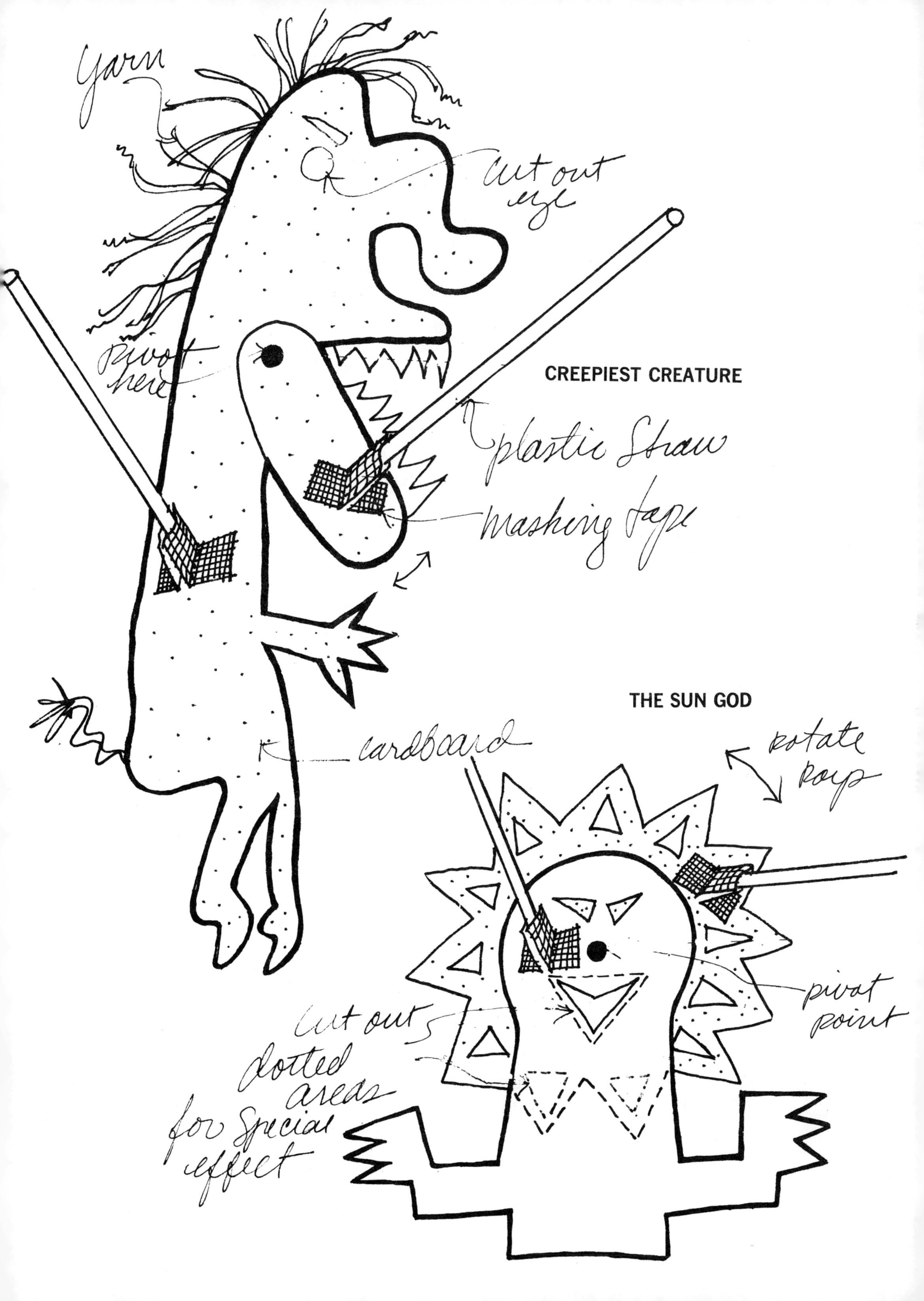

CREEPIEST CREATURE

THE SUN GOD

Abstract Puppets

This unusual technique is not only fun but particularly worthwhile when looking for a fresh approach in finding a story. Based upon the Rorschach test concept of finding forms in abstract inkblots, this project helps students' imaginations to soar, as they explore areas of unsuspected richness. Furthermore, it is a marvelous enhancement of language-art skills in story development.

Beginning the Project

Divide the students into teams of three. Together, discuss the kinds of lines they might use to draw shapes—curved, twisted, zig-zagged, wiggly, angular, and so on. Give each team a sheet of colored poster board and ask them each to draw a shape which utilizes the *entire* cardboard. After they have finished drawing, have them cut out the shapes and study them carefully, to see what forms they suggest. A shape might be an animal, a person, a creature, inanimate object, landscape or anything else that comes to mind. It might be one thing to one observer and a completely different thing to another. Let the students linger over the shapes for a while, possibly writing the names of the images they see on the backs.

Creating a Story

Now let the teams start thinking of a story idea, using their three shapes as characters, scenery, or props. For example, one team might have shapes that suggest an old castle, a six-legged bear, and a strange bicycle. The challenge here is to create a story around such unlikely story elements; students will have great fun pitting their imaginations against these abstract images. At this point, the story could be developed into either an improvisational outline or a written script.

Constructing the Puppets

Once the students have established ideas of the characters or props they wish to construct from their imaginary shapes, have them begin to transform these shapes into puppets or final constructions. Colored paper, scrap fabric, straws, paper cups, paper plates, and throwaway junk are excellent materials for creating textures and features. Legs, arms, ears, etc. may be added. Shapes can be split apart, say at the jawline to make a movable mouth which uses paper fasteners as pivot points. Or in another modification, several students might decide to link their shapes to create a more complex puppet, scene, or prop.

To enhance the atmosphere of this creative time, play some lively music while the children work on their puppets.

Operating the Puppets

Children are adept at discovering the many ways these puppets may be manipulated. Some shapes (such as a piece of scenery) work best standing up and need not be moved at all. For others, the type of staging used will partly determine the way the puppets will be maneuvered. In a traditional window-type stage opening, for instance, they may simply be attached to rods and held from below the opening. Or perhaps they will be hung from strings and handled in a marionette fashion over a table top with a stand-up set. A more liberating technique is to use the entire floor or any open area as the stage. Students can simply hold the puppets in traditional Japanese Bunraku style, gripping extended cardboard pieces added to the backs, or they can even attach the shapes to their bodies with string and become the puppet themselves.

Expanding the Project

A project such as this one allows the leader tremendous latitude in experimenting with different combinations and approaches. Use the freedow to encourage imaginations to soar! The results promise to be interesting!

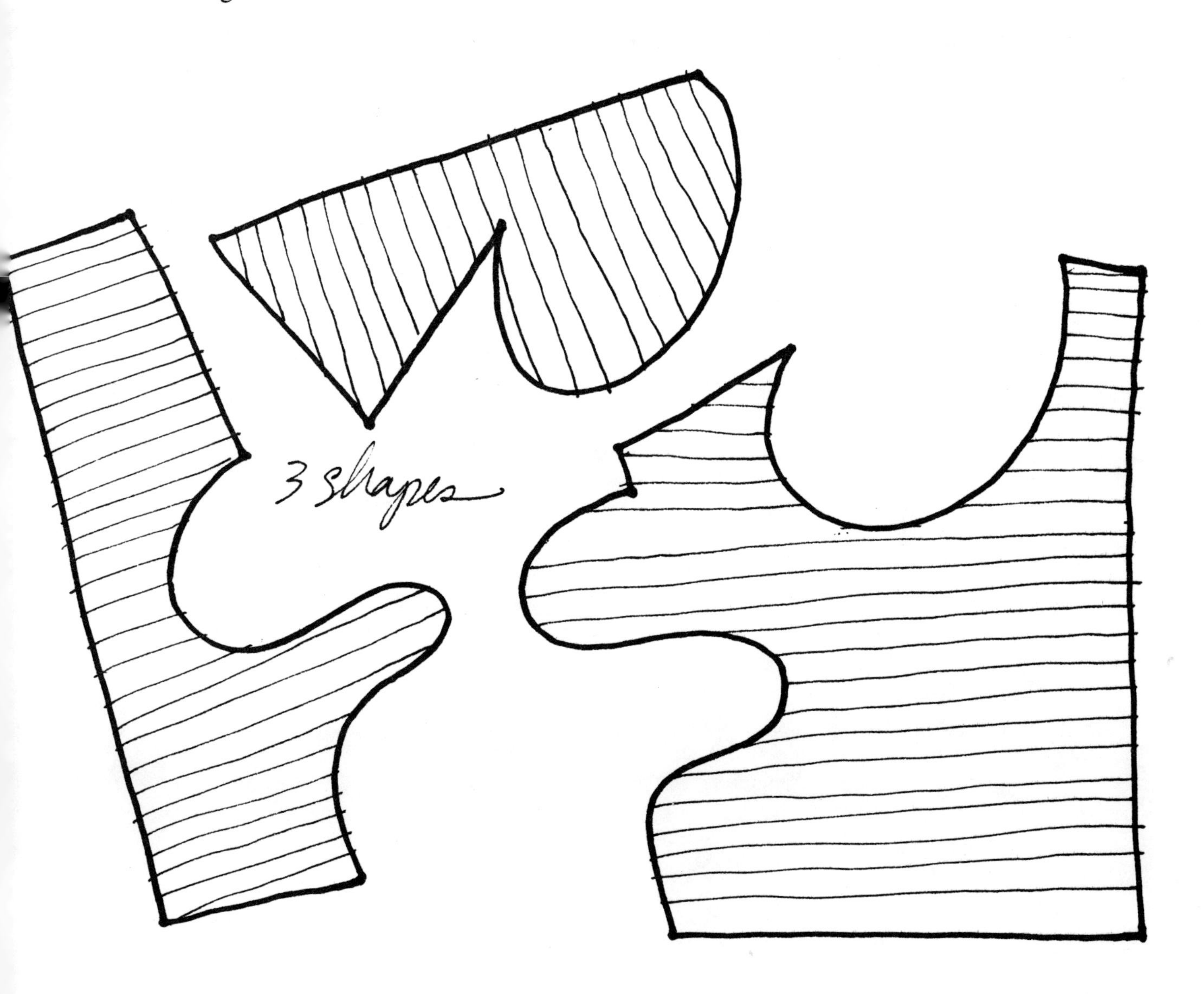

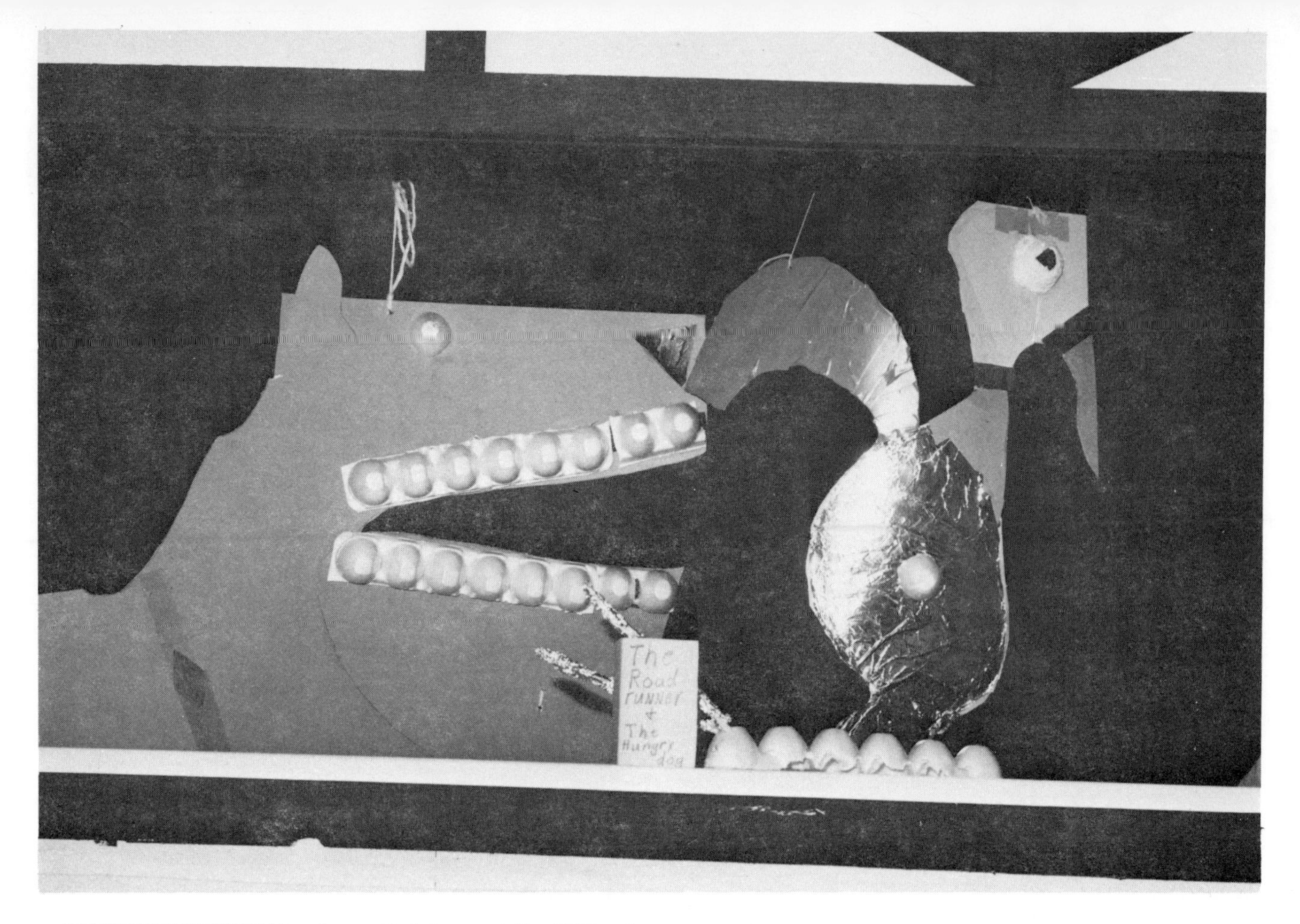

ABSTRACT PUPPETS—Jason Palafox and Jim Willemin
Dog and Bird

ABSTRACT PUPPET—Kim Travis
Sea Monster

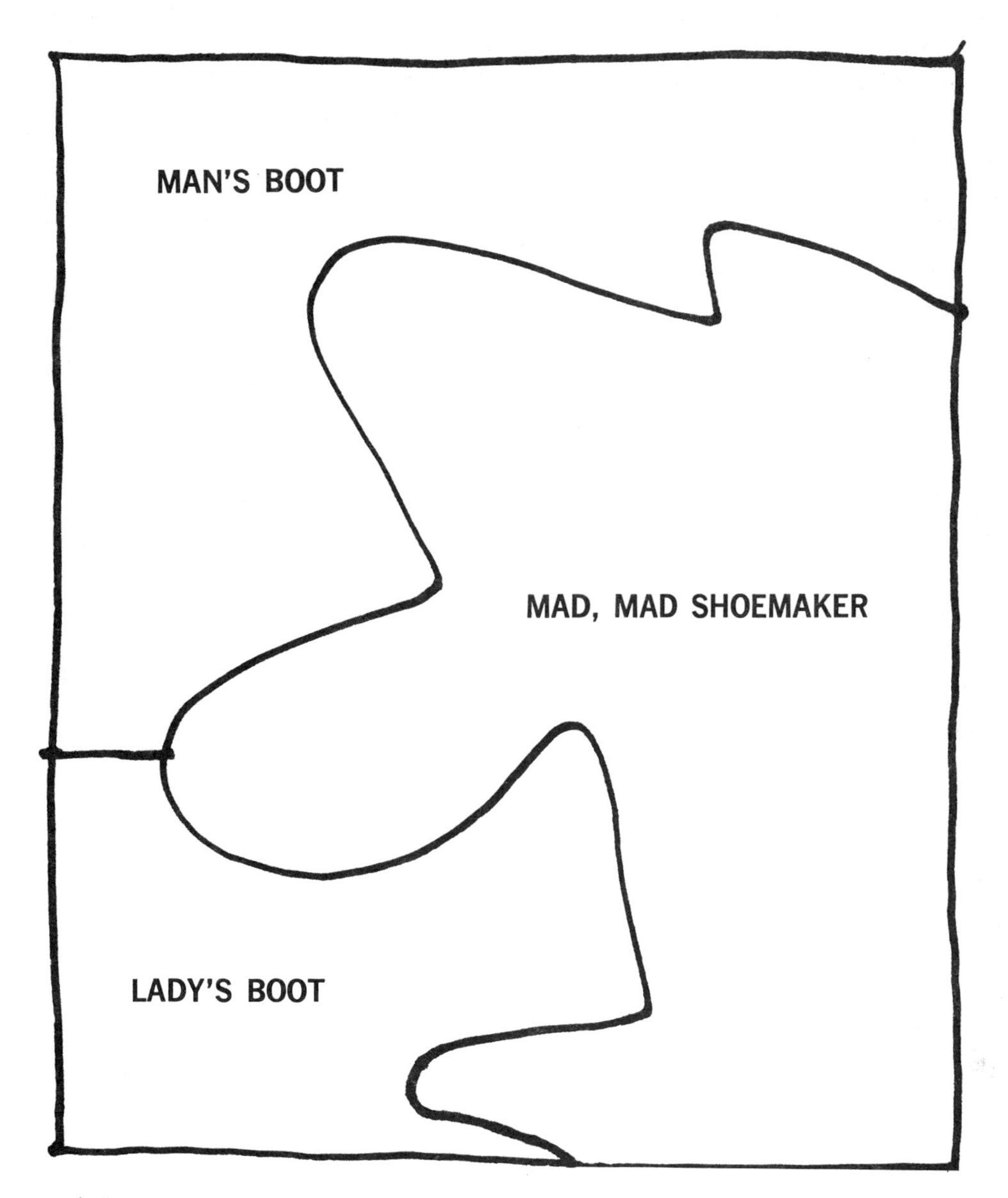

these three shapes
cut from a single sheet
of cardboard, comprise the
cast for a puppet production
(see following page)

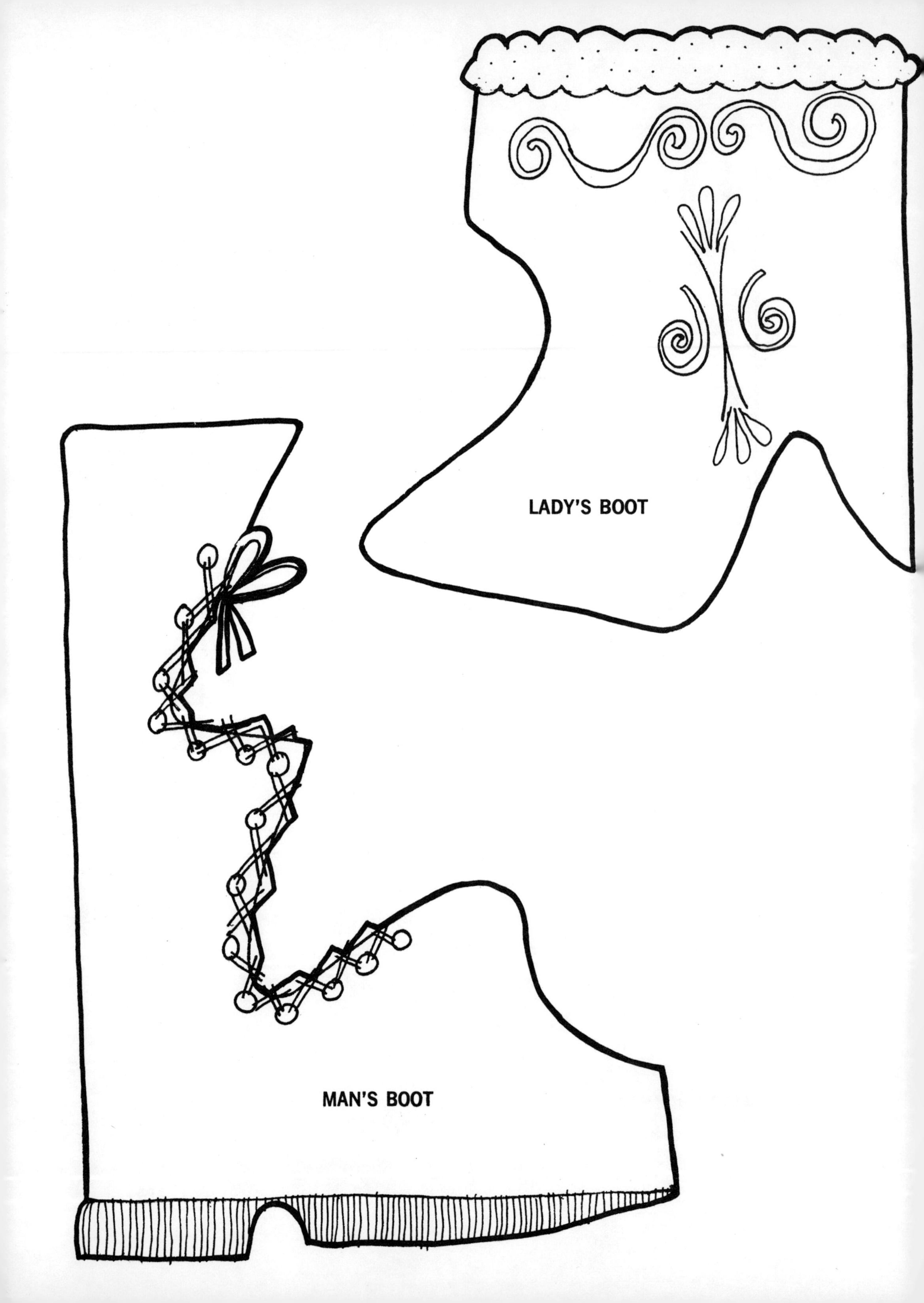
LADY'S BOOT
MAN'S BOOT

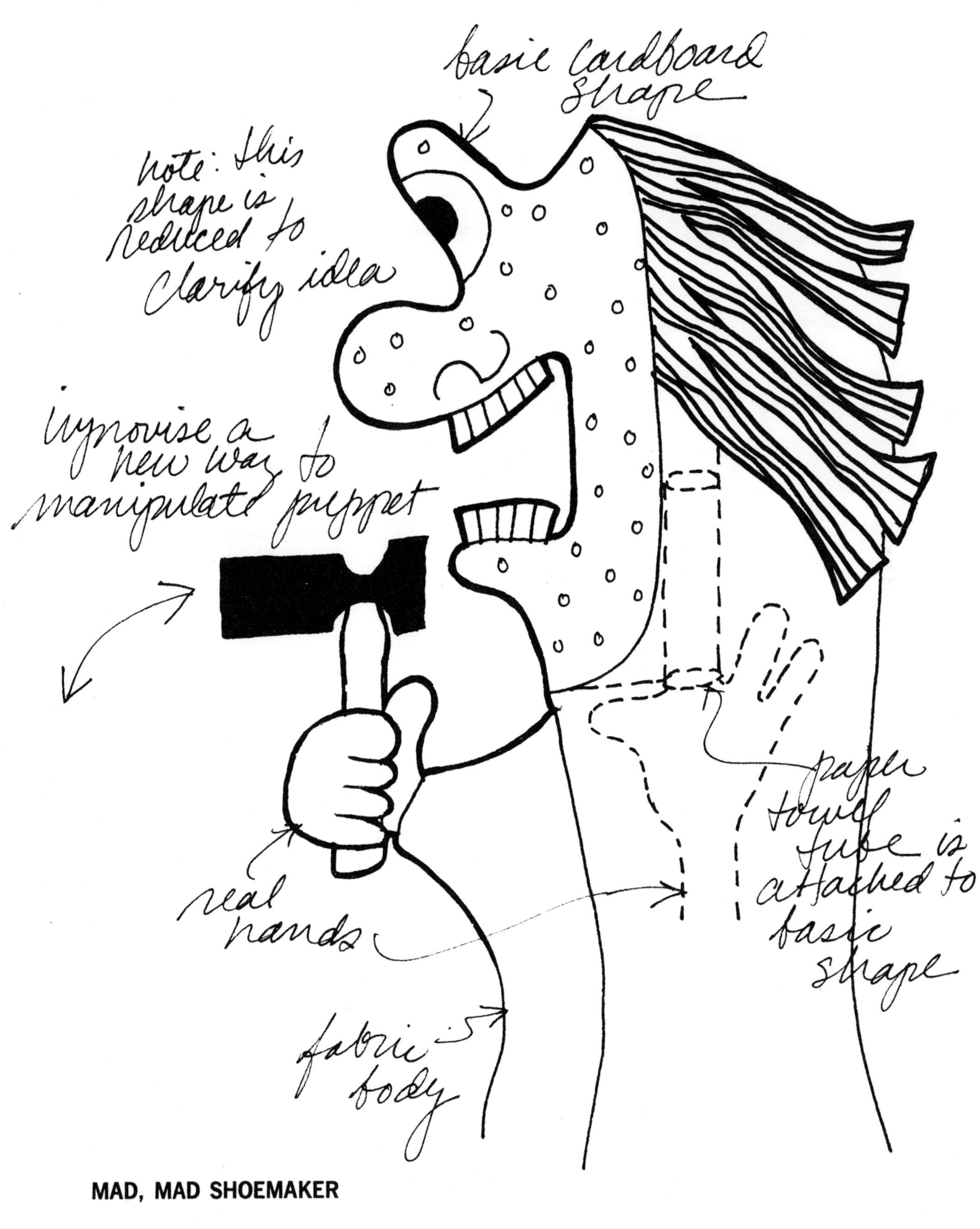

MAD, MAD SHOEMAKER

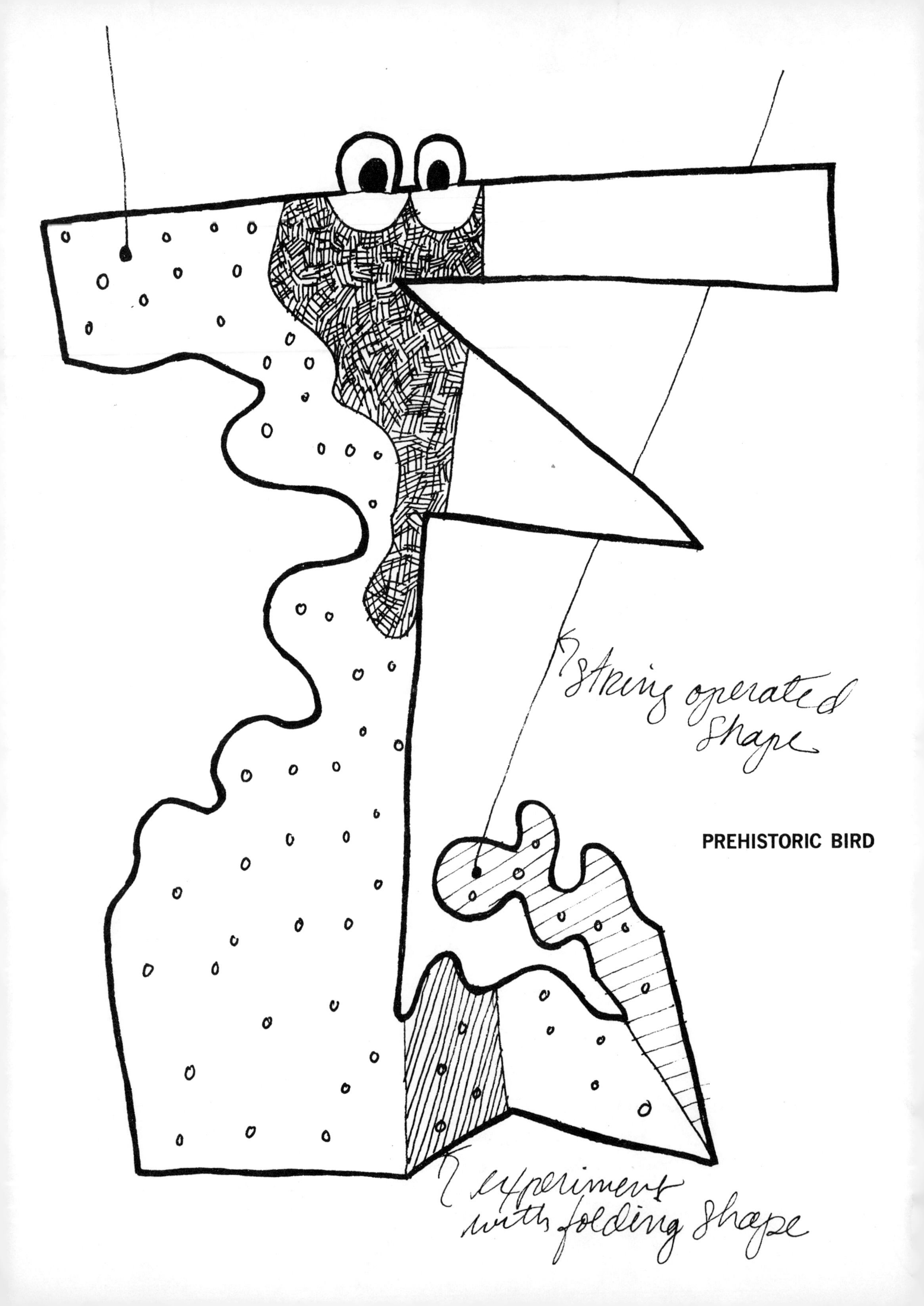

PREHISTORIC BIRD

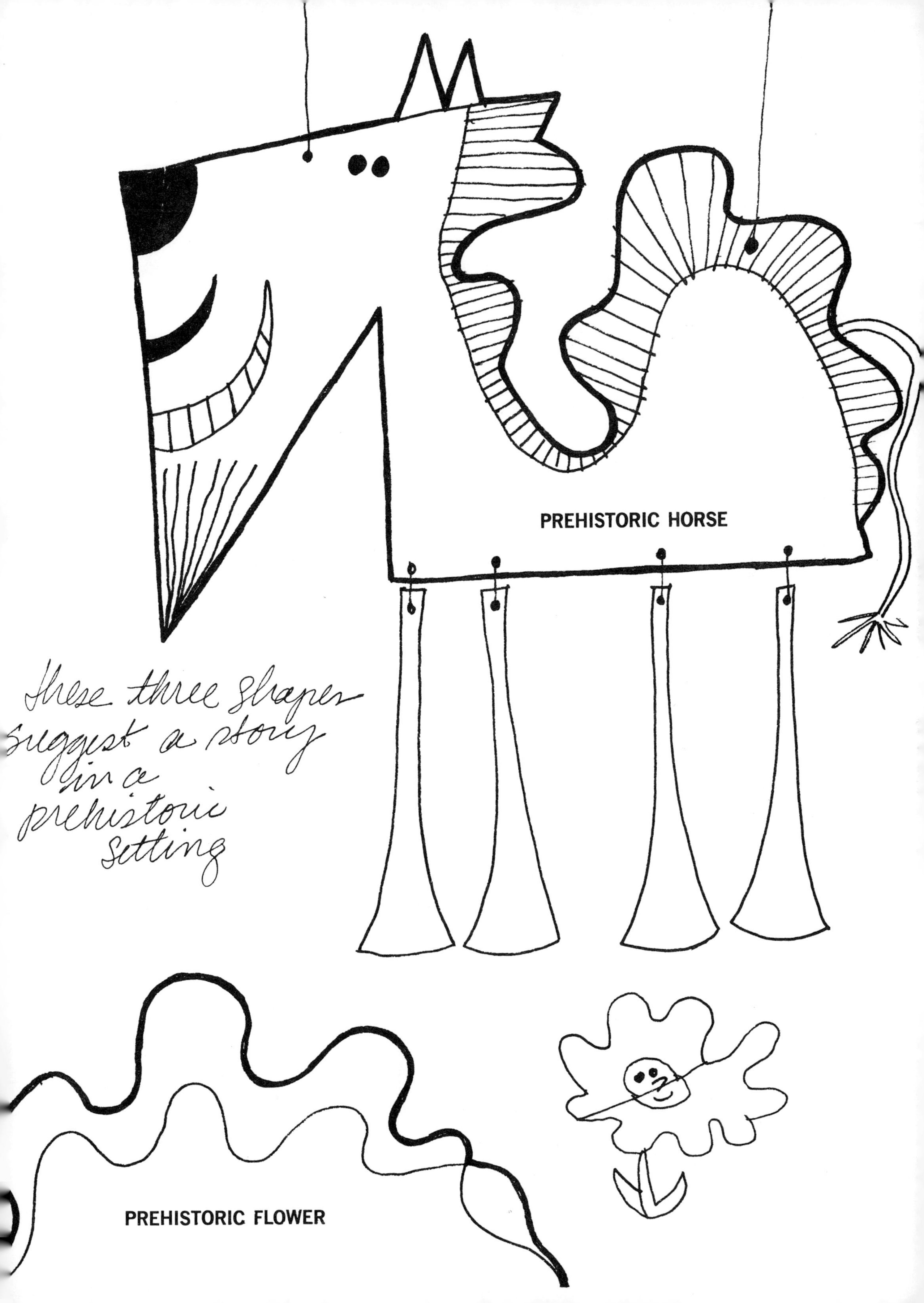
These three shapes
suggest a story
in a
prehistoric
setting
PREHISTORIC HORSE
PREHISTORIC FLOWER

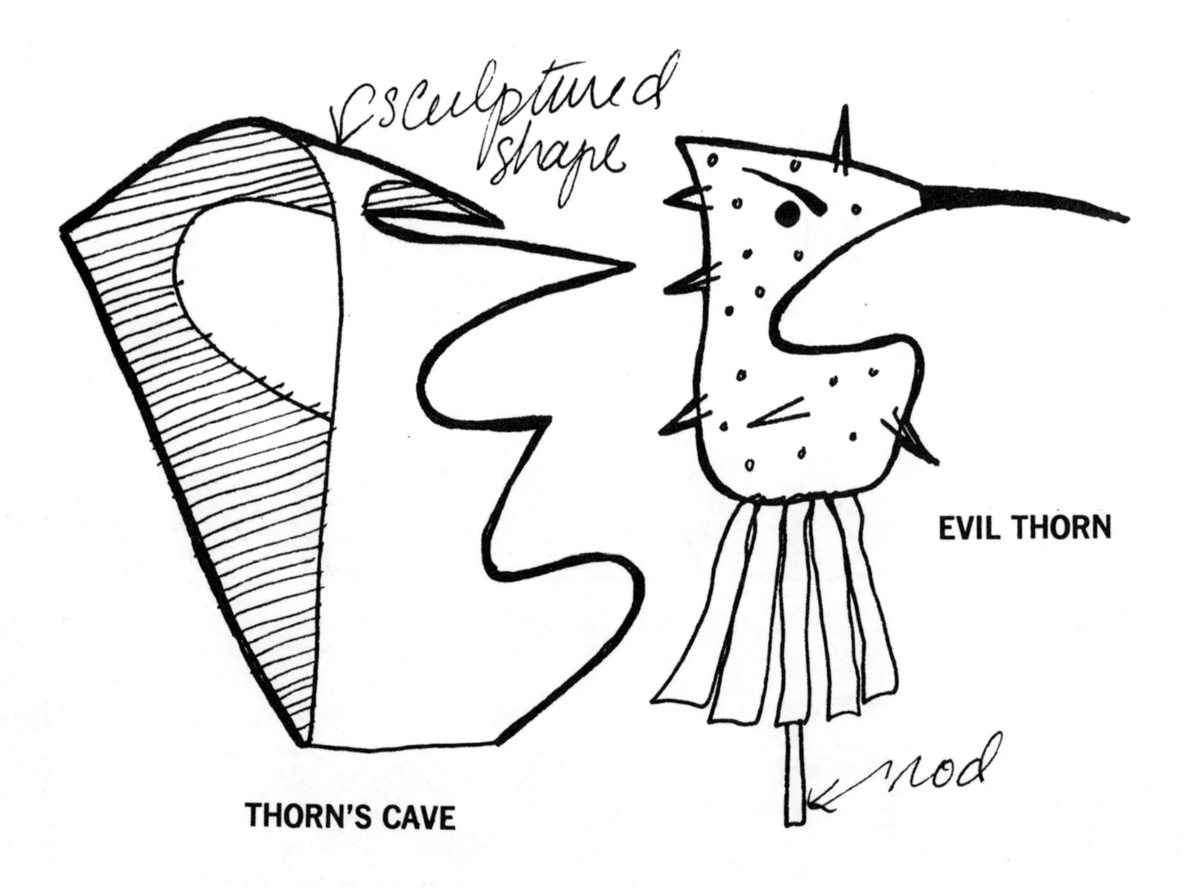
sculptured shape
rod
EVIL THORN
THORN'S CAVE

these three shapes
evolve a story plot
around an
evil character
and a
good
character

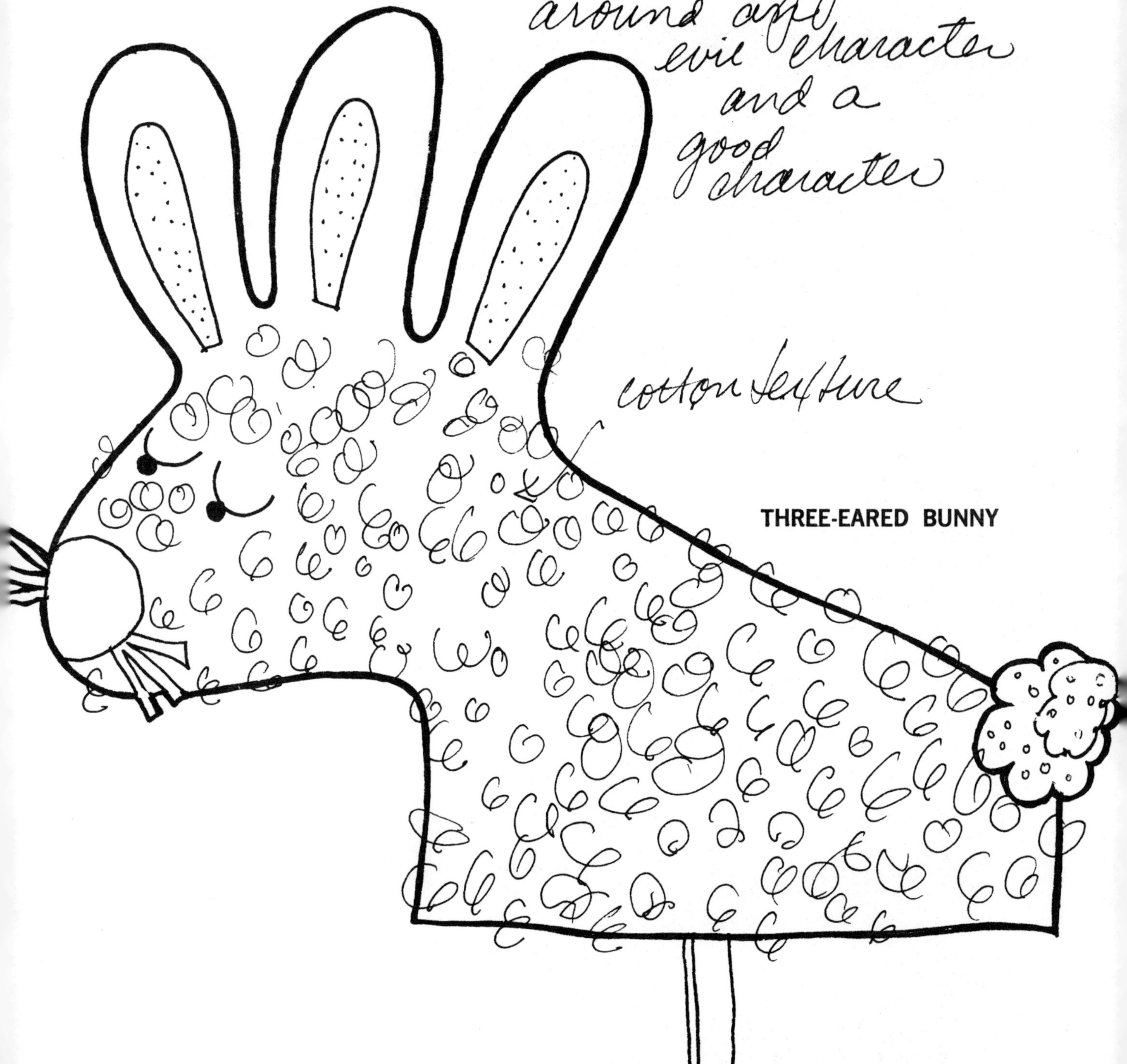

cotton texture

THREE-EARED BUNNY

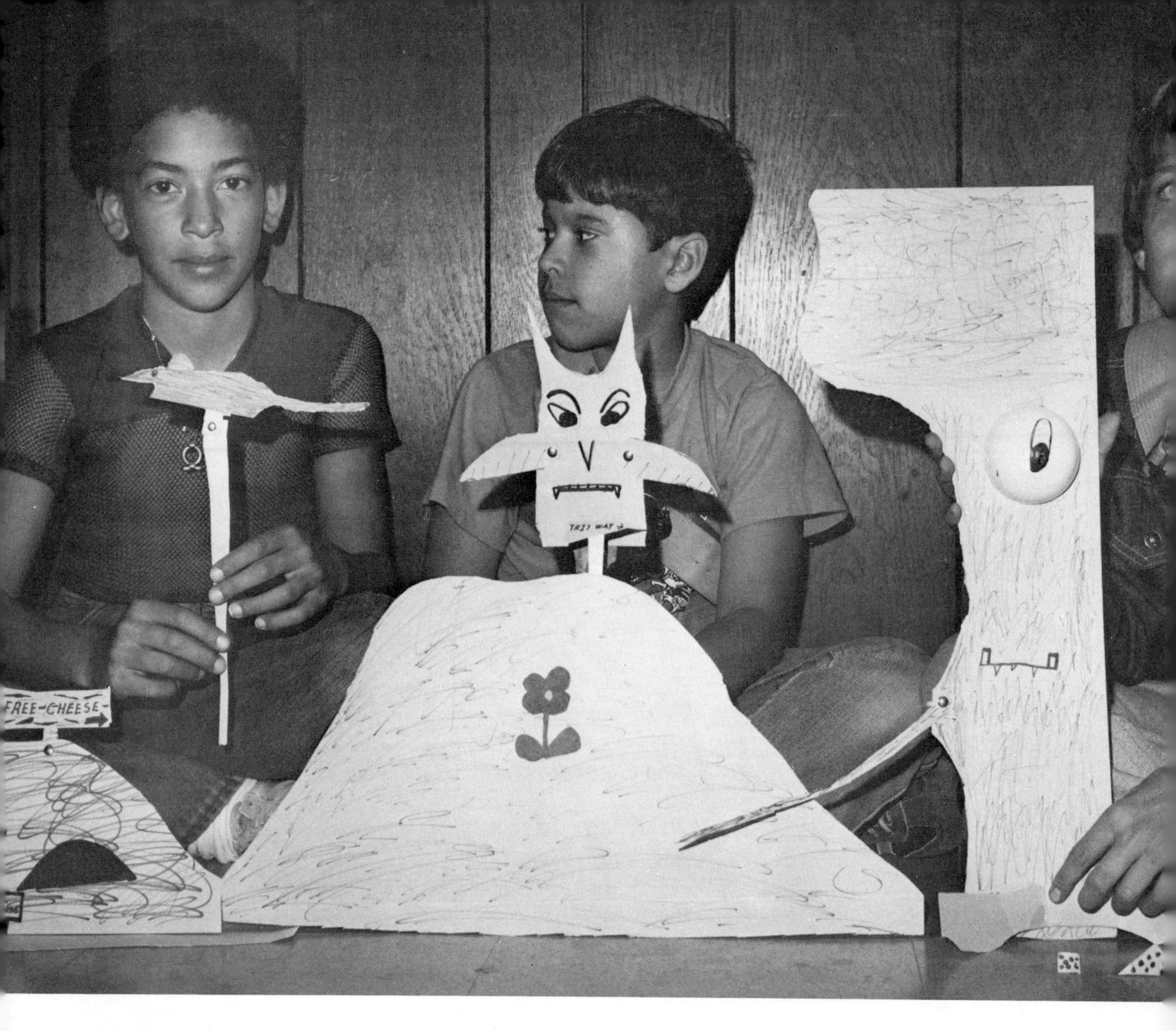

ABSTRACT PUPPETS—Kevin Wilson, Stony Toquay and Danny Mangold
Mouse, Owl and Tree

Body Puppets

These large animated creatures hang from a cord around the neck of the puppeteer and cover the entire front of the body. To allow more control over the puppet's movements, its wrists and feet may be fastened to those of the child. These puppets are highly dramatic creatures which all children would enjoy.

Body puppets are excellent for deaf children, whose own hands may act for the puppet in signing the story. The children should learn to sign *around the puppet's face*, rather than the child's. However, I have also seen children successfully using their own faces for signing, rather than the puppets; thus one might want to experiment with both methods. Blind children could also explore this unique concept by developing textured body puppets that could be "felt" by other children in a hands-on theatrical experience.

Constructing the Puppets

The following drawing, a typical body puppet developed at the Texas State School for the Deaf, is a good basic one with which to begin. Its large detergent-box body, which makes the puppet particularly lightweight to carry around, "floats" the paper-plate head out away from the body. The limbs must be lightweight and flexible enough to insure free movement and should be securely attached to body. These puppets will undergo a great deal of stress by the children in action if not properly secured, they will fall off; therefore, it is important to secure joints with ample masking tape, silver electrical tape, glue or staples, beforehand.

Other materials can be explored for creating body puppets. For example:

Heads—could be from cardboard cut-outs, boxes of various kinds, or paper plates.

Bodies—from cardboard cut-outs, loose fabric, clothing such as old skirts, dresses or shirts, giant-sized detergent boxes, supermarket paper bags.

Limbs—from stuffed recycled stockings, cut-off sleeves from dresses or shirts, pant legs, simple strips of fabric, or loosely rolled newspaper covered with fabric or crepe paper.

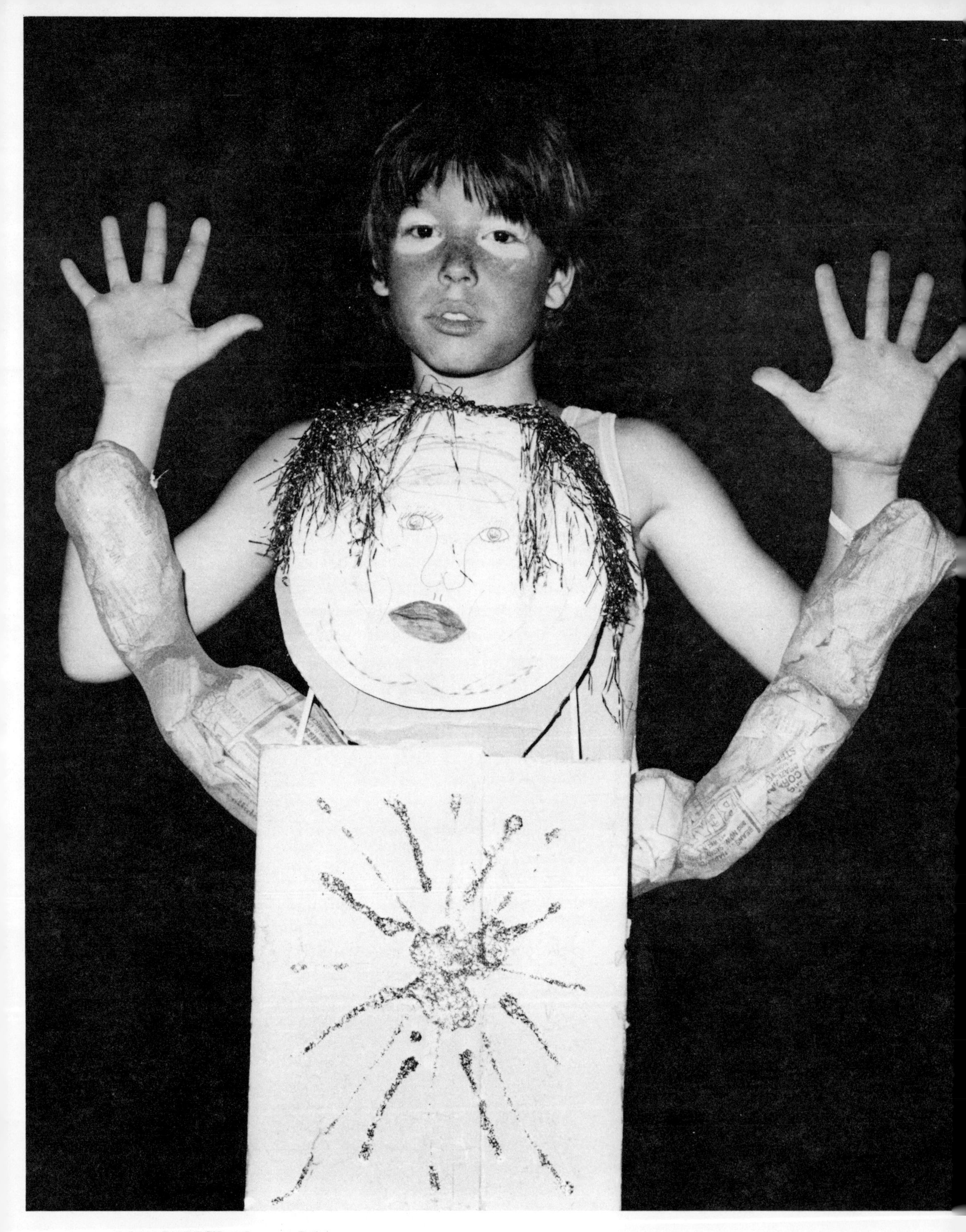

BODY PUPPET—George Zein

paper plate
neck strap
large detergent box
elastic band
rolled newspaper covered with fabric
nylon stocking stuffed with wadded newspaper
sew elastic bands on legs of puppet to attach to childs' ankles
* attach limbs securely to box

MOUSE

Cardboard Bunraku Puppets

Bunraku is a traditional Japanese form of puppetry which is unlike that of any other country in the world. It is capable of achieving a high level of sophistication in both design and manipulation. The Bunraku characters are large in size, allowing the puppeteer to hold the puppet forward in performing (which is done by gripping a control device on the back of the head.) In Japan, a trio of puppeteers operate various parts of a single puppet. This same technique can be adapted to modern puppetry utilizing one or more puppeteers.

Constructing the Puppets

A basic Bunraku puppet's body and head can be constructed by cutting out large pieces of grocery-carton cardboard (such as appliance boxes). Loosely cover the body and head sections with large sheets of grocery bags; staple the bags to the cardboard pieces around the edges, leaving a small area open to stuff. Stuff stapled bag sections with wadded newspaper then staple remaining edge together. Arms and legs can be made from strips of fabric, old sleeves, pant legs, knee socks or recycled nylon stockings. Add cardboard hands and feet to limbs.

Operating the Puppets

Decide which parts of the puppet will be manipulated and improvise hand grips on the backs of head, hands or feet with cardboard, wire, wood or other material, as shown. Hold puppet securely in a forward position above the floor, and experiment with movements, such as yawning, waving goodbye, raving in anger, etc. Try a tarantula, snake or many-legged octopus, using many operators.

Bunraku performances are ideal to perform in an open space or on a theater stage. Because of their size they can easily be seen by a large audience. Stand-up scenery assembled from large pieces of cardboard are ideal to use with these puppets.

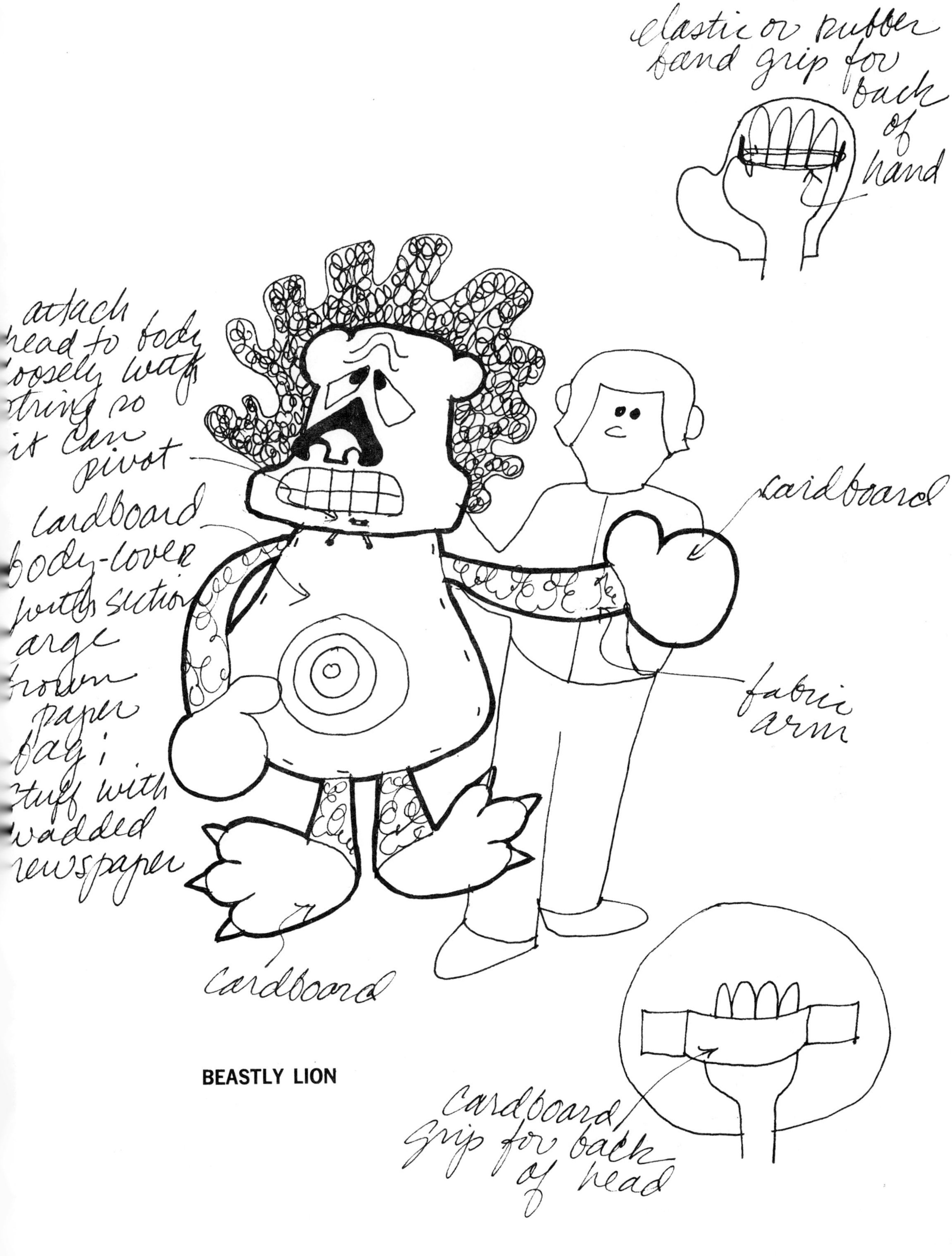

elastic or rubber band grip for back of hand

attach head to body loosely with string so it can pivot

cardboard body-cover with section large brown paper bag; stuff with wadded newspaper

cardboard

fabric arm

cardboard

BEASTLY LION

cardboard grip for back of head

CARDBOARD BUNRAKU PUPPET—Harvey King
Pizza Chef

BUNRAKU PUPPET, VARIATION—Laura Lyon
Spider

AN OP ART PUPPETRY EXPERIENCE

by Judith Schwab, art teacher

With electronically synthesized music, "Kosmos," as my accompaniment and an extraordinary Op Art puppet swinging freely, I entered my fifth-grade art class. A cellophane strip dangled from its head—attached to the strip was a bell! Paper-fasteners joined body and neck to head. Its arms were folded paper and it owned no mouth or nose. The students were ecstatic with this bizarre creature and cast votes to select an appropriate name for it. The winning name was "Orbit-Zornit." As Orbit-Zornited to eerie electronic music, it, too, made its own unique sounds. Orbit-Zornit's instant triumph provided a provocative introduction to concepts of color theory.

Op Art can be defined as any nonobjective arrangement of line, shape and color that creates an illusion of three-dimensional space on a two dimensional plane. Color complements can "work" for an artist to subdue a color or create the effect of colors advancing or receding. Since most of my students could not identify primary, secondary or complementary relationships, the combination of Op Art and puppetry proved to be a valuable and exciting tool for teaching color theory which also allowed experimentation with a wide variety of materials.

Joseph Albers' *Homage to the Square* and Richard Anuszkiewicz's *Plus Reversed* were two of the many valuable resources on color we used, thus taught us, for example, ways to create illusions of "vibration" by juxtaposing complementary repeated patterns of red and green. One class period was used to view slides of the Op Art show, "The Responsive Eye," held at the New York Museum of Modern Art in 1965. We dissected one-point perspective and showed how three-dimensional depth could be created by converging lines. The students brought examples of Op Art and geometric illusions cut from magazines or taken from gum wrappers. We discussed examples of Renaissance floor perspective, showing how each generation builds upon lessons from other generations. Many new words were added to the students' vocabulary. They were excited to try some Op Art designs of their own.

They were given graph paper, mechanical drawing tools, and a choice of any two complementary-colored markers. Breaking a circle into shapes and segments of color was an exercise used to create the appearance of depth and space. The students quickly became familiar with complementary colors by working with them and discovered that one can not always trust one's senses.

After the Op Art compositions were completed, we were ready to construct the puppets from a resource bin of colored cellophane, foil papers, popsicle sticks, rubber bands, ribbons, multicolored telephone

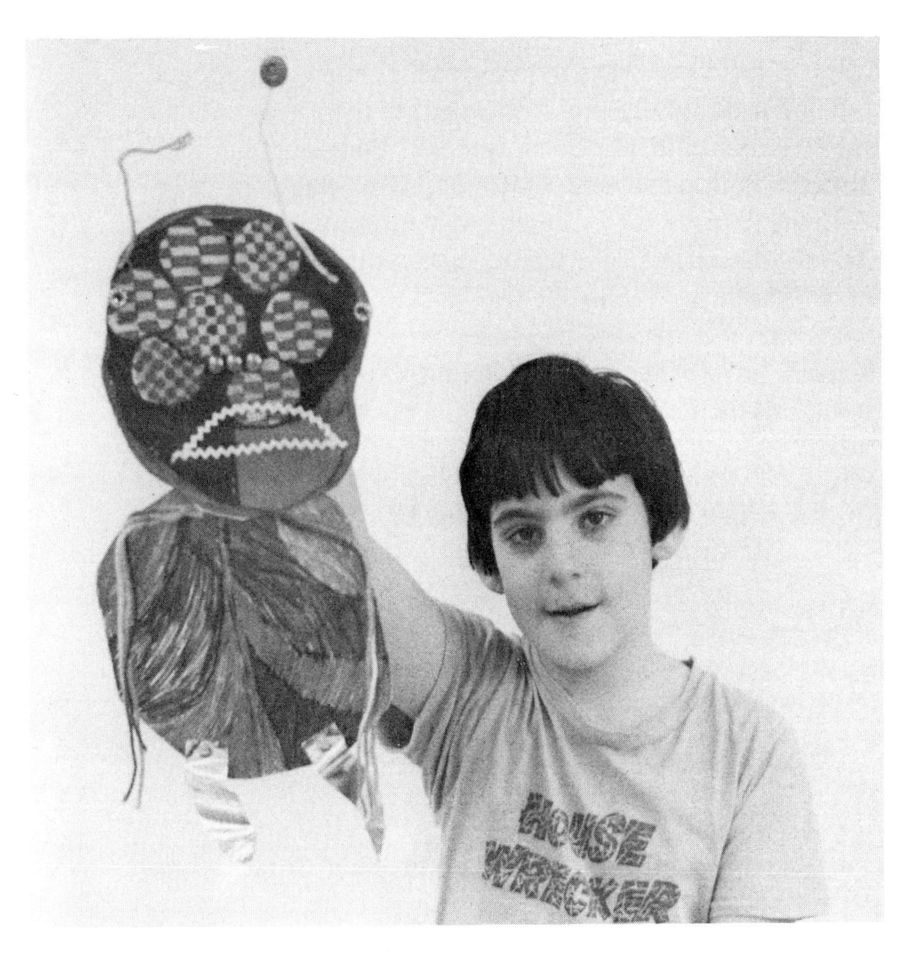

OP ART PUPPET—David Lishelberg

wire, paper fasteners, and many, many other throw-aways. The basic puppet was made from oak tag paper. The Op Art designs were the basis for puppet ideas and were converted into head, body or other parts. I showed the students how to fold and coil paper to make curls and springs. I emphasized that *every* part of their design was important.

Most students worked with two design ideas: one inspired by the work of Joseph Albers, another by the work of Bridget Riley. They were asked to devise a creature never seen before. It need not have such human characteristics as arms, head or body; it could be whatever the student wished it to be. They were asked to consider the creature's "basic" needs, such as:

—*How does it move from place to place?*
—*How does it experience sensual stimuli? Does it have eyes, noses, feelers, or antennae?*
—*What kind of sounds does it make?*

The students chose a variety of ways to activate their Op Art puppets. Some stood behind and used rubber bands attached at the top to saucily ricochet them about the room. Still others operated their puppets with rods in front of a screen with scenery projected from an opaque or overhead projector. Moving scenery was created by painting with dyes and magic markers on acetate sheets, overlaying one with the other and moving them back and forth.

After the puppets were completed, the students, working in groups, expanded their learning experiences by developing short stories in their language-arts class. The theme, as one might guess, was outer space. One such story goes:

IN A GALAXY FAR, FAR AWAY

by Andrew Hoffman, age 11

There was a space-age family called the Orbits. The Orbits lived on the planet Op Art. They had 24 illusions in their family. They were *all* very modern, considerate and very good looking. The family was quite happy until the gang, Non-Complementary Color, came and invaded them. All the Orbits scurried as fast as they could and hid, except one Orbit. This Orbit was the bravest of all. Non-Complementary Color took him and ran off with him. The brave Orbit was never seen again.

The students produced a number of shows, all on their own, and invited other classes to the premiere. Not only did they make the puppets and write the plays, but they became directors, actors, scenic designers and technical directors as well.

Judith Schwab is a graduate of Kean College with a Bachelor of Arts degree in Art Education, and is a teacher in the Manalapan-Englishtown school district of New Jersey.

rubber bands secure child's hands to the puppet

puppet animated in front of child's body

try different ways of manipulating the puppet

puppet held on stick in front of screen on which scenery from the opaque or overhead projector shines

AN UNDERWATER SETTING

Table-Top Theaters

Table-top theaters offer a simple staging technique with a different perspective. Georgian State Librarians explored these two types shown. One allows the audience to take on a birds-eye view while standing around the table; the other presents a frontal-view for a seated audience. Marjorie Batchelder delves into this type of approach in her classic book *Puppets and Plays*.

TOWN SETTING

TABLE-TOP PUPPET

WITCH

PUPPETRY FOR THE SPECIAL STUDENT

Physically Disabled, Hearing and Visually Impaired

PUPPETRY FOR THE SPECIAL CHILD

Physically Disabled, Hearing and Visually Impaired

by Nancy Renfro, adapted from Puppetry in Education Newsletter, January 1979

I have been partially deaf all my life, and it seems that much of my time was spent overcoming the problems of this handicap. Although I have never thought of myself as handicapped my "survival" stemmed from (was contingent upon) a deep commitment to creative activities.

It was pure chance and good fortune that brought me together with the East Campus, Texas State School for the Deaf in 1978. The immediate enthusiasm and warm reception from supervisor Sue Drake and librarian Marion Granberry drew me, ironically, into a totally new world, because being partially deaf is not nearly the same as being totally deaf.

Sue and Marion were eager to hear about new techniques in puppetry for the deaf. Since the conventional talking-mouth puppet was not suitable for the deaf, a new type of puppet was needed; thus the body puppet was developed. Out of my brown bag came a sample, comprised of two paper plates for a head, attached to a long cardboard body and fabric arms and legs. This large puppet would be worn around the child's neck and attached at the wrists and ankles with rubber bands, thus enabling the child to use sign language while operating the puppet.

The first day in Marion's class with the deaf was quite poignant; I was not prepared for these joyous and wonderfully animated beings. Since our culture inhibits body language and tends to restrain hand movements the constant movement of hands and body in this classroom was refreshing. Total communication should be more than small movements of the mouth alone. The teaching and encouragement of sign language, drama, dance and rhythm should become an integral part of our educational system. From the handicapped we could learn that disabilities might well be considered gifts.

We introduced our first puppet project to two third grade classes; they produced puppets and scenery for Maurice Stendak's *Where the Wild Things Are* and Fritz Weaver's *A Voyage with Jim*. The students created large body puppets, paper-bag animal heads, cardboard mice and sea-life marionettes, mostly from throwaways. Rhythm teacher Cynthia Roup devised "growing trees," to add another dimension to the production, that of body movement. Within eight weeks the two productions were ready and excitement ran high throughout the school. To be on the stage, to know the glory of performing, was a most important event for these students. Anyone, including the disabled, need opportunities to feel important, to reach heights as performers, artists, and achievers.

The stage is a fitting avenue in which to release their vast reserve of energy. The turning point of the show occurred when a young girl who rarely spoke surprised everyone by reciting her two lines loudly and clearly. We realize, at times like this, the value of puppetry.

Puppets are an extraordinarily valuable tool for the teacher of the special child—the hearing and visually impaired, as well as the child who is physically or emotionally impaired. Unfortunately, the true potential of puppets has barely been tapped. It is time for educators to rethink their methods, and to boldly explore ideas which may spark entirely new learning experiences for the special student. Although the scope of this book cannot adequately cover such a vast and important field as puppet therapy, the chief aim of this brief section is simply to introduce some new ideas. *The key to working with unconventional children is to use unconventional puppets.*

THE HEARING IMPAIRED

Puppets capitalizing on sign language, such as the body puppets shown in this book, have proven successful with the deaf. Puppets with flexible arms and heads (but without talking mouths) as well as rod, string, and shadow puppets are excellent in allowing hearing-impaired children to take part in pantomime and "body language" stories, with or without a narrator/interpreter. Puppets with strong visual impact, such as the stuffed-paper-rod and cardboard Bunraku puppets are also quite effective.

The stage could be open areas in the classroom, theater or gymnasium, to allow maximum exploration of movement.

THE VISUALLY IMPAIRED

An obvious area of exploration for the visually impaired is texture. Large puppets made from a variety of textures—yarn, paper, tin foil, plastic wrap, cotton and of course, fabric would play an important role in portraying characters with tactile qualities. Since speech constitutes a huge proportion of their daily life, the visually impaired would particularly enjoy puppets with large talking mouths.

The stage as well as the puppets should be nonconventional. An audience might be requested to "feel" the play taking place in a *rope theater*. Such a rope theatre is an open area which has been roped-off so that blind performers may use the rope to orient themselves with scenery and the other characters.

A visually-impaired audience might participate directly by using these same ropes during the performance.

THE PHYSICALLY IMPAIRED

Puppets should take into consideration the limitations of the physically impaired. A child with little use of the hands might simply wear an immobile mitt-type puppet, designed not to come off easily. A wheelchair-confined child could take advantage of the "table-top theater" idea shown elsewhere in this book. Or a portable stage built from a cardboard grocery carton could enable the child to have a traveling theater.

Special puppets could be designed to encourage physical therapy. Exercises for the hand muscles could be enhanced by a five-finger glove with faces on the ends of the fingers. Similarly, a snake puppet worn over the entire arm could develop weak arm muscles in a more enjoyable way than more typical therapy.

USING PUPPETRY IN SPECIAL EDUCATION

By Joy Magezis, adapted from Puppetry in Education Newsletter, 1978

QUESTION: What are the various ways puppetry can be used in special education?

ANSWER: Puppetry can be used as a therapeutic tool in all areas of special education. Because it is such a freeing and open-ended media, its possibilities seem limitless. Here are a few areas where puppetry has been used to great effect.

Puppetry and the Blind

Blind children or adults can construct papier mache heads and cloth bodies themselves and achieve a great sense of accomplishment. A puppeteer that I knew, who is now blind, feels that the puppets he has made since losing his sight are stronger characters than those he made earlier in his life. Blind people tend to make more precise puppets. For example, small cracks in a puppet head are more noticeable to blind people, who make better use of their sense of touch. By first painting the head a skin color and then using masking tape to define where the mouth and eyes will be, the blind person can even paint in the facial details.

The blind can manipulate their puppets and produce a show with directional help from the sighted. They soon catch on to stage directions and the correct hand and arm movements.

The blind can enjoy attending puppet shows if they are given the opportunity to feel the puppets before or after the show. Of course, shows with a lot of dialogue are best. If the sighted are performing for a small group of all blind children, the performance can be done in the audience. The audience can sit in a semi-circle with the arena in the center considered the stage. The blind can be given the opportunity to touch the puppets at various times during the show.

Puppetry As Physical Therapy

Puppet construction demands muscular usage and and motor coordination. Construction techniques can be designed according to the specific needs of a patient. The therapist should choose the kind of puppet to be constructed that will necessitate the use of the appropriate muscles.

Coordination between hand and eye is advanced by all methods of puppet-making. Development of hand muscles can be achieved by making papier mache heads or cellu-clay hand or rod puppets. Any kind of puppet can be modified to meet certain specific needs. For example, if you want to make a paper-bag puppet with a child who cannot use a scissors, different shapes can be pre-cut from colored paper and the child can paste these on the bag to create desired effects.

Puppet manipulation also stimulates muscular development. Puppets can be manipulated in many different ways (depending on the type of puppet constructed), thus meeting the needs and limitations of the different patients. The muscles of the fingers or hands can be developed with finger or hand puppets. The muscles of the lower or upper arms can be developed by using a puppet whose mouth opens and closes.

It is so much easier to practice using specific muscles if you can enjoy yourself and communicate at the same time.

Puppets and Speech Therapy

Puppets motivate children with speech difficulties to speak as clearly as possible. For many children whose stuttering is caused by emotional problems, puppetry is a wonderful outlet because fluent speech is often achieved when they use puppets. Children with other speech problems will try especially hard to have their puppets understood.

Since hand and eye coordination is often related to speech problems, puppet-making and manipulation, which improve general muscular coordination, can be especially helpful.

Puppetry in Psychological Therapy

When a child uses puppets to create a spontaneous, individual production, a constructive emotional outlet is provided. The child can express inner conflicts, problems, desires and fantasies without having to immediately take direct responsibility for them and without being physically exposed. The puppet provides a socially acceptable means of releasing pent-up frustrations and anxieties.

Many play therapists have found puppets more useful than ordinary dolls because of their adaptability to role playing and the way in which a child can freely disappear behind the personality of the puppet.

When the child uses puppets in role playing, the child's problems can be acted out and possible solutions can be tried. These puppet shows will help children gain new perspective on their problems.

There is also therapeutic value in having a child watch a puppet show performed by others in which a puppet works through and solves a problem. Another technique to try is to have the puppets themselves present a problem to the audience and then ask the children to work out a solution. The show can be stopped and group discussion held.

A positive group experience can be created by having the children produce a puppet show together. In order for the children to make a good show, they have to cooperate with each other. An excellent opportunity is provided to discuss and stress constructive criticism. The actual performance of the show provides a special kind of group experience for all children. If a child does not want to perform, she or he can still participate in other ways, such as making scenery, doing the lighting, etc.

There will never be a lack of material for discussion if the child and/or therapist use puppets. A discussion can be started after a child has seen a show performed by others simply by asking the child to retell the story. Therapists can use a puppet to direct or enhance a discussion.

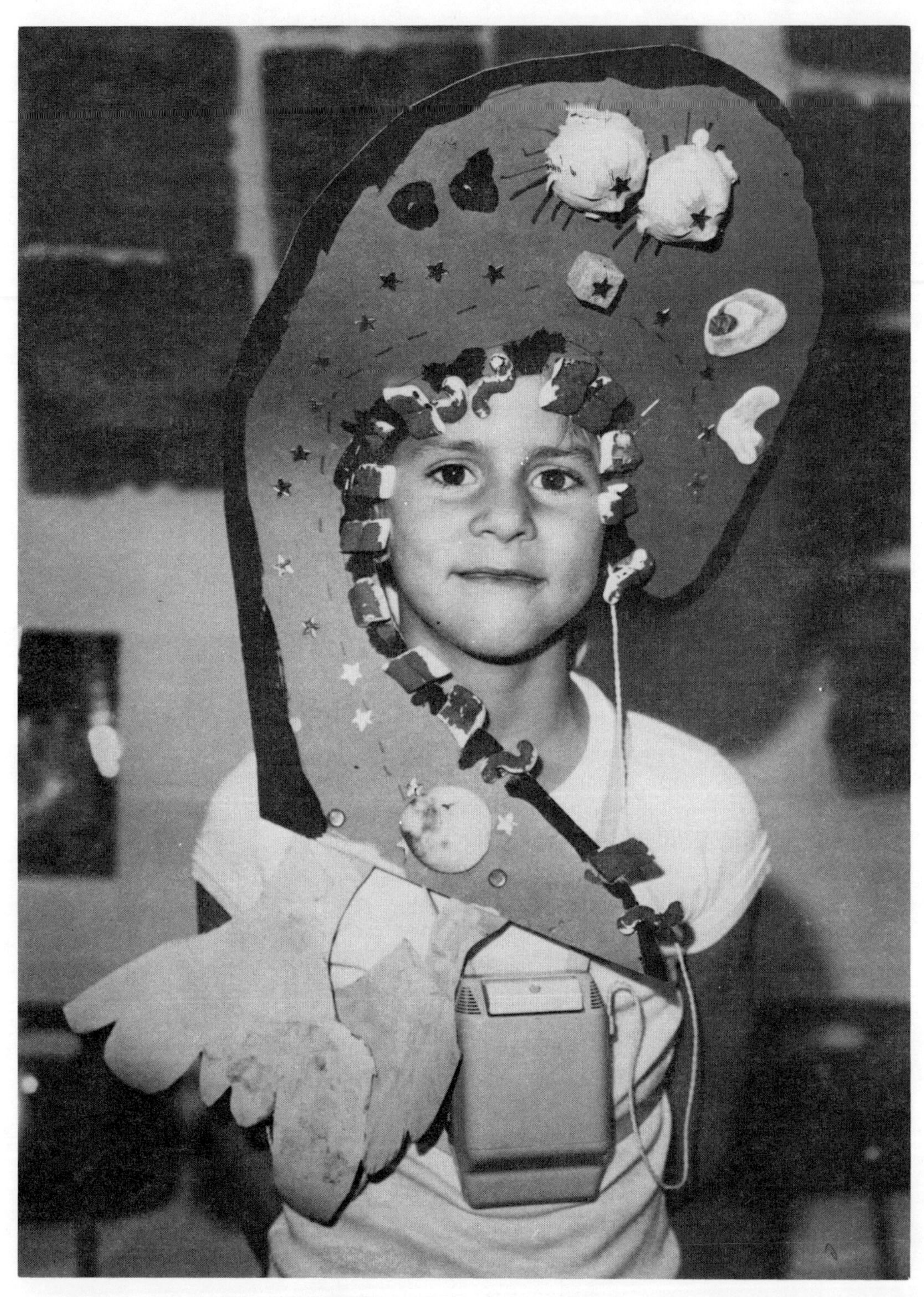

ABSTRACT PUPPET—Brandy Otto

AN ABSTRACT PUPPET EXPERIENCE

by Cynthia Roup, Rhythm Teacher, Texas State School for the Deaf

My motivation for employing the use of abstract puppets with young deaf children ages 6-9 was for them to experience kinisthetically the relationship between movements and sound.

I was attempting to expose the children to the fact that particular sounds evoke certain expressive movements; for instance, a sound played on a metal xylophone would suggest a different mood and hence movements than the sound of a loud and irregular drum beat.

The process of making these abstract puppets demanded social skills, group support and cooperation as well as individual creativity and ingenuity.

These puppets were very simple and inexpensive to make. Materials were provided for decorating, painting, making features and adding other odd ornaments to the shapes. These characters did not have to be defined—what was emphasized was how that character was identified through its particular movement and sound. The abstract puppets were tied to the child's body. The child was given free time upon completion of his puppet to dance, to move and to experience his creation. Creativity is a way of finding new relationships through physical exploration and indeed this is what happened when the kids donned their creation of an abstract body puppet. Some children had their faces hidden behind the puppet; one even had a two-face puppet, mother and father, expressing both of them through her own movement and chosen sound.

A large array of musical instruments were lined up in the room and the children listened as each instrument was played by the instructor. They became acquainted with each sound for a new purpose: they were to choose which sound best portrayed the characterization of their puppet.

They explored the different instruments and chose a friend to accompany them as their abstract puppet danced to the musical instrument of their choice. New dimensions of creative movements blossomed through abandonment. Steady flute music brought out a flowing dance movement and a staccato wooden xylophone sound was interpreted through the staccato type dance. It was then clear to the children that relationships do indeed exist between two elements of movement and sound.

Speech development brings the children into a relationship with the outside world whereas music brings the children to a more personal relationship with themselves. This experience is especially beneficial to the deaf child who is so visually oriented, with his major mode of learning being visual. It has become necessary for the development of a more "whole" deaf child to give him these experiences of relating to sound, music and movement in a freely creative and unthreatening manner.

ABSTRACT PUPPET—Lenny Kuehne
Bird

ABSTRACT PUPPET—John Dabney

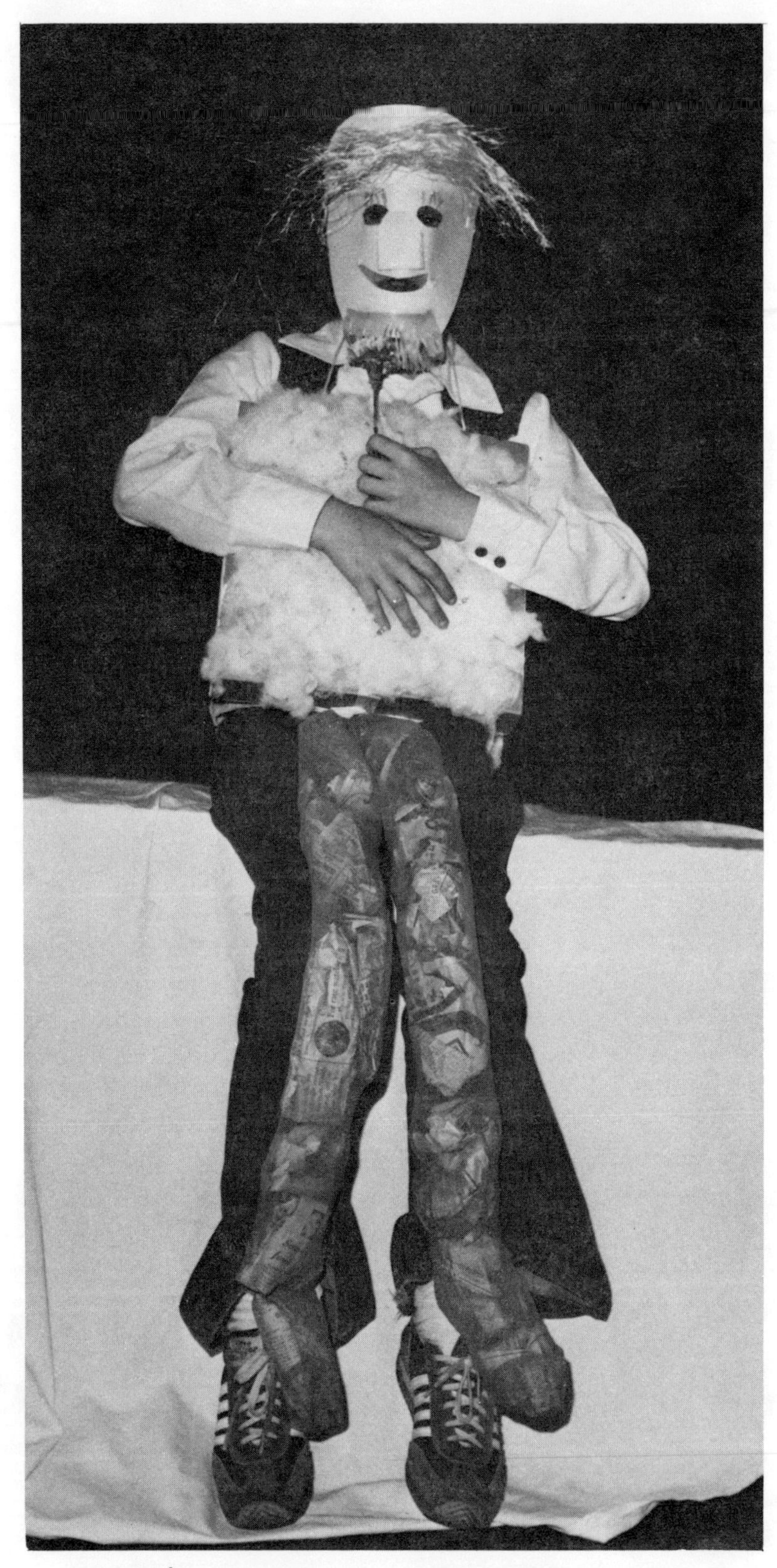

BODY PUPPET, VARIATION—James Petrosky
Angel

BODY PUPPETS FOR NATURAL LANGUAGE DEVELOPMENT

A STORY FROM A PAINTING

by Cynthia Roup, Rhythm Teacher, Texas State School for the Deaf

The purpose of these puppets was to approach the development of creative language through the avenue of the creative arts. Instead of building a language story through the typical linguistic mode, the choice was made to initially create a story through the intuitive mode of thought.

The project began by having the class do creative, interpretive movements, first to music which was described as light, easy, pleasant flowing, heaven-like and then to heavy dark, low, evil, bad-like music. The following day the class was divided in half and each group was given mural paper and tempera paint. The assignment was to use the paint to portray the same feelings which were evoked through the music, the heaven-like quality and the evil-like quality—the age old theme of good vs. evil. Only color, form, and movement of lines were used to portray these two qualities. Everything was abstracted. No pictures were drawn. The children discovered that the bold primary colors of tempera paint had to be "toned down" by mixing colors to depict the light quality. Upon completion each mural was examined and "word" impressions were listed on chart tablets to describe the mood, action, thoughts, feelings and setting of the good and evil mural. This established a vocabulary of nouns, verbs, adjectives and word phrases, providing a skeleton for the story.

The process of building a story was then discussed. The children agreed with the idea that a good or happy story meant that pleasant, happy, friendly and good deeds are used to help solve the main conflict or problem in the story, thus creating a good ending; vice-versa for the evil story.

The children voted first to build a story based on the "good" mural and related vocabulary words. They went to the library and browsed through books that had happy endings, since this defined the children's concept of a "good story." They recalled such classic stories as "The Ugly Duckling" and "Cinderella."

A class discussion in total communication was then held in order to create our "good" story. The children referred back to the listed vocabulary. These words served to initiate and motivate ideas of characterization, mood, setting and story plot. Children's ideas were combined to comprise different scenes in the story. And with much ease the stories unfolded to the amazement and satisfaction of both students and instructor.

Another mural was then drawn to illustrate the new story. This time the characters and settings were the prominent features. Upon complet-

BODY PUPPET—Edward Mott
Villain

BODY PUPPET—Eric Smith
Sun

ion, each child chose the character he wished to portray and created his life-sized body puppet based upon his ideas of what he had learned about the character through this process. The puppets were made predominately from various size boxes and old hosiery stuffed with newspaper and decorated with concoctions of materials generously donated by fellow teachers.

One story's setting was heaven and employed simply props of clouds— A little angel was sad because he wanted to join the angel's musical parade being held in honor of crowning a new boss of the heavens, but he was rejected by fellow angels because he had no talent for playing a musical instrument. The problem was resolved when the good dancing angel showed the little angel how to dance. He was then accepted into the parade and all were happy.

The younger class based their story on *Hansel and Gretel.* The poor girls and their mother worked hard. Mother became sick and hungry. They had no food so the two daughters went to the forest to find food. They met an evil man but refused his offer of candy. They came upon a beautiful gum house where the good queen lived. She gave food and magically changed their rags to riches. She guided the children back home, aided the mother, leaving them with good food, nice clothes and a new house.

This process of building language from the abstract mode has proven to be very successful from these experiences. These children collectively participated in a fun, creative, and educational project that children from other classes, witnessing this process, have expressed their eagerness to also experience.

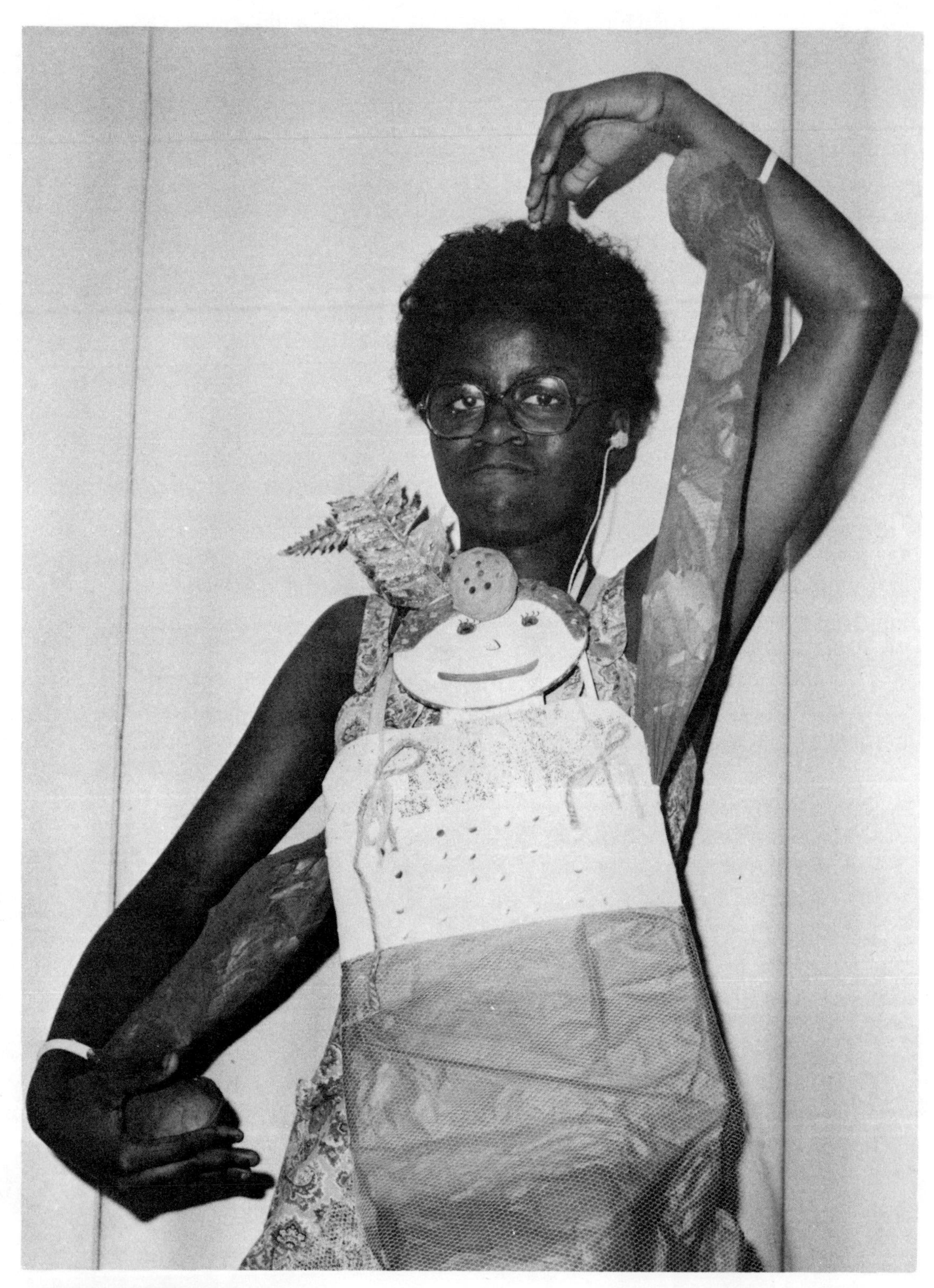

BODY PUPPET—Marge Evans
Ballerina

BODY PUPPET—Denise Kuehne
Good Fairy

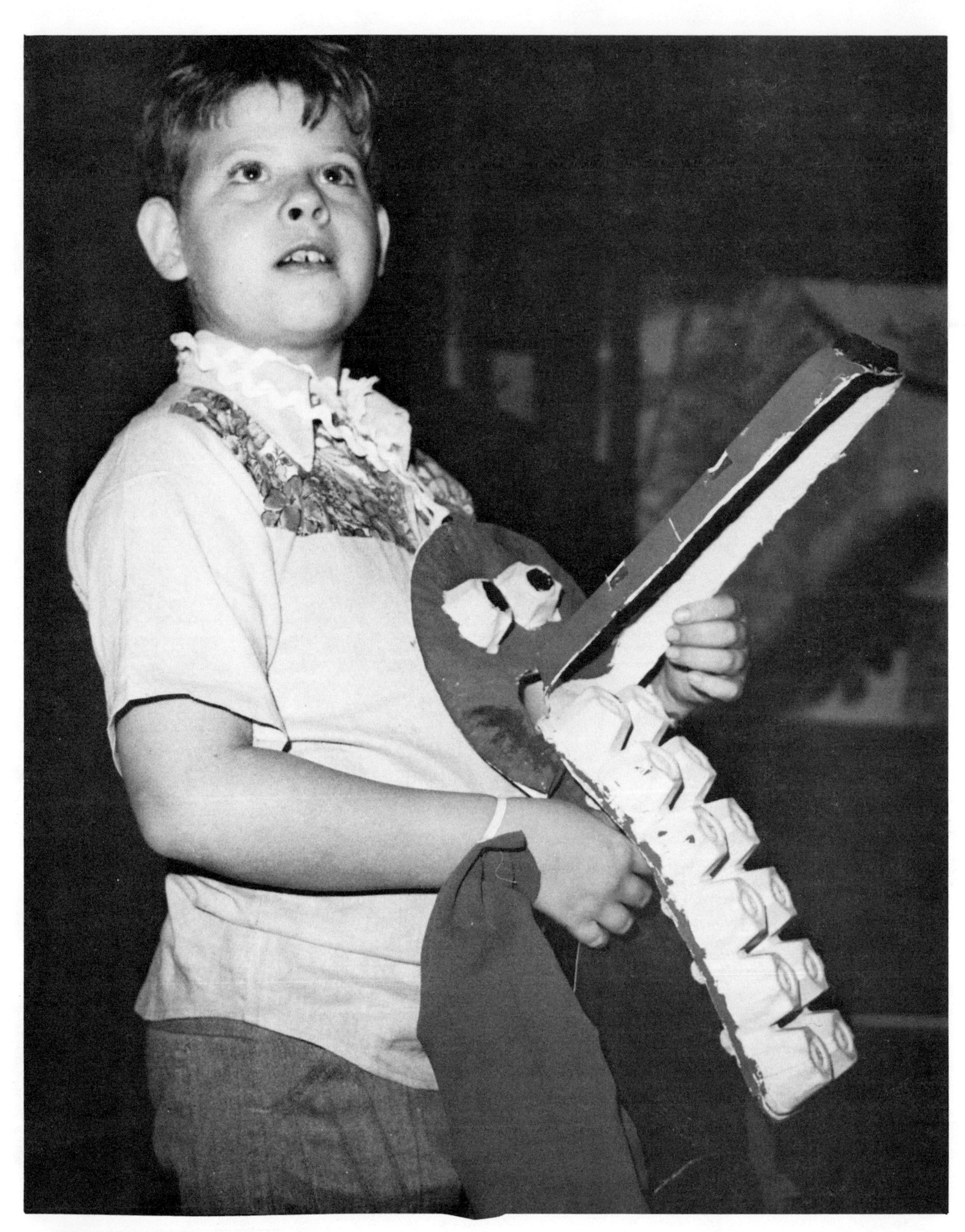

BODY PUPPET—Keith Burleson
Alligator

STORY-TELLING THROUGH PUPPETRY WITH BODY PUPPETS

by Marion Granberry, Librarian, Texas State School for the Deaf

There are important factors that children need to learn about stories. By choosing a story and translating it into a puppet show, many of these factors may be learned in a more creative way than simply reading a story and discussing it.

First, each child must choose the character he or she wants to play—establishing the main characters in the story. Then they must study the physical and emotional qualities of their character. Making a puppet that will match the personality and the way the child perceives his character is a creative and educational process. Sometimes the child will study other similar characters, as when portraying animals, in order to make it more authentic. For example, Keith was making a squirrel. When looking at pictures in other books, he noticed that the two front teeth were always prominent, so this became an outstanding feature of his puppet.

The child must study what his character says, how it feels, the cause and effect of its actions, and how it relates to the story as a whole. Through dramatization, a reliving of these factors of the story, a growing understanding becomes an expression of the child himself and is internalized. The puppet itself sometimes is a less complicated method for children than acting with their own bodies. The paper bag or paper plate or box comes alive in the child's imagination and he himself does not have to change to the character.

The vocabulary in the story must be understood thoroughly for effective portrayal. Researching the meanings and concentration games are helpful in mastering the vocabulary. Even rewriting the story in the students' own words and using their script for the production is a method of internalizing the story's language. Pictures of their practices, with the script beside it, are excellent reading exercises and review.

The mood and setting of the story are essential factors. To recreate these elements is an artistic challenge and a problem-solving situation. How would you make a boat that sails on the ocean? The children covered a roller cart with blue paper and made a boat that sat on the top.

The memory of sequence of events in the story is necessary for a final production. Reviewing the story bit-by-bit, sequencing pictures from the story, and making a miniature stage out of a cardboard box with paper stand-up figures are ways of learning the order of actions beyond the simple rehearsal process. Sometimes changing the ending or a part of the story in practice helps to emphasize what actions should be remembered and serves as a release from the tedium of the rehearsals.

The production is ready, and quite often the dress rehearsal is far

BODY PUPPET—Lisa Boren
Bunny

from perfect, but the children always pull through for the final performance. The reward of the applaud and bows outshadows the fun of creating the puppets, but when those children pick up that book the understanding and the fun will flow back into their memories. And when next they hear a story, they will relate to with new enthusiasm and with knowledge of the factors that comprise a story.

They are not the only ones to benefit. The audience has been given the entertainment of seeing a story come alive in a unique and imaginative way.

This approach for story telling may be applied for both hearing and deaf children. The problem one finds in deaf children giving a puppet show is that traditional puppets used in America are ones that fit on their hands and the stage is a small stage where only the hand puppet can be seen. The children without very good and loud speech must rely on someone to talk for their puppet, and if it is an audience with any deaf people watching, the interpreter must sign for the puppet. The puppets are limited to action and some emotions.

The body puppet frees the hands of the deaf for signing and their mouths for speech, yet still retains the properties of puppetry. In the process they expand the puppet stage and open the way for more imaginative and creative movement.

In relation to story-telling, these particular kinds of puppets offer special experiences. Their large size makes them more easily seen by a larger audience. For young children the skills of cutting, pasting, and gluing are more easily mastered than sewing and the larger features are easier to create.

The fact that these puppets attach to the body requires body movement and language which are a part of total communication. The child can walk his puppet on the stage. Although the child can be seen, as with Japanese Bunraku puppets, the body does not distract the attention away from the puppet. It is as though the child becomes one with the puppet.

Props, such as chairs and tables, etc., may be used with this larger puppet as well as more elaborate backdrops, adding a more realistic touch to the play. The expansion to open space allows more children to participate in a show.

Story-telling in the form of puppetry has now taken on a new dimension.

BODY PUPPET—Lynn Boren and Terry Harris

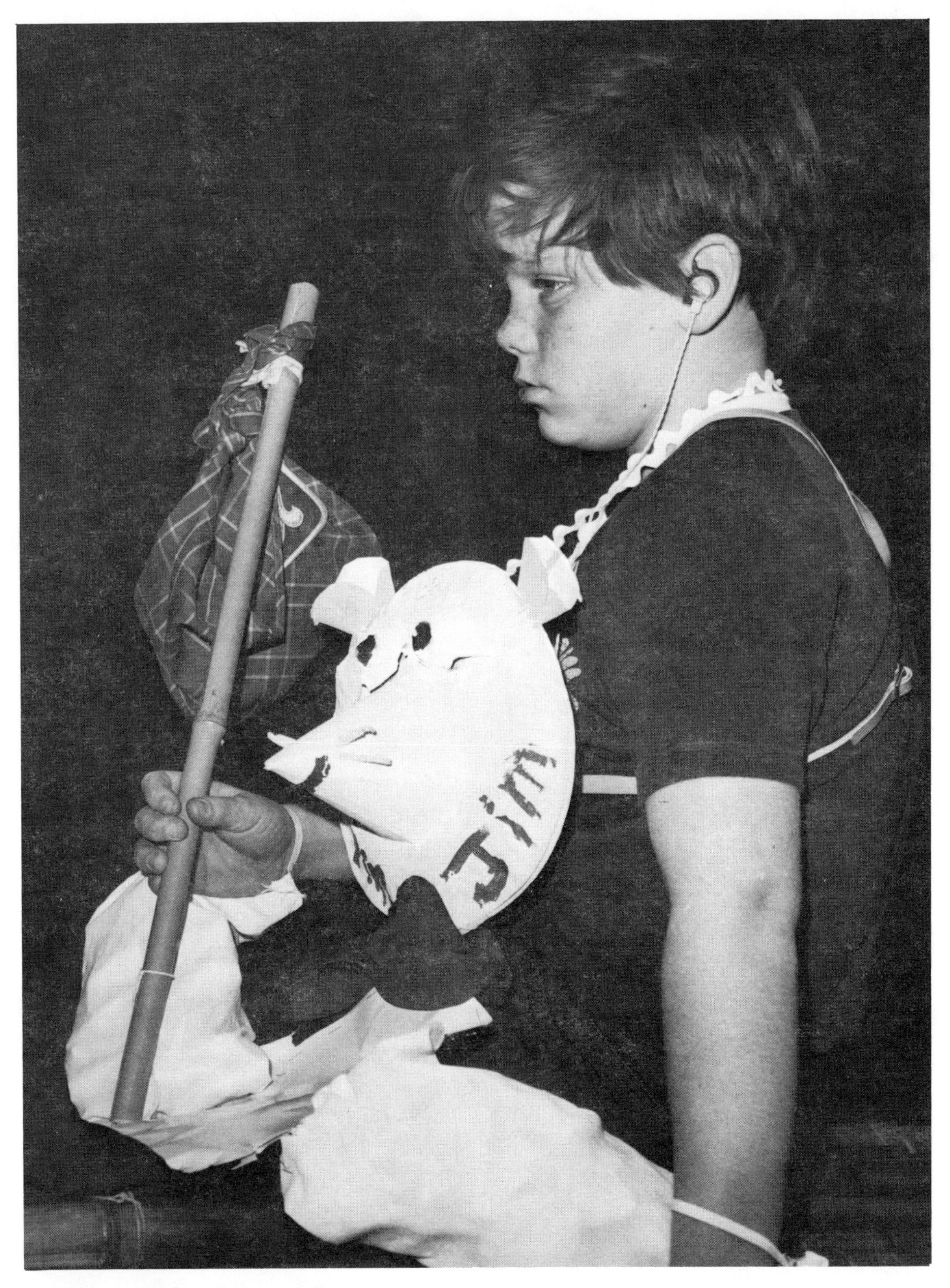

BODY PUPPET—Sammy Oats
Mouse

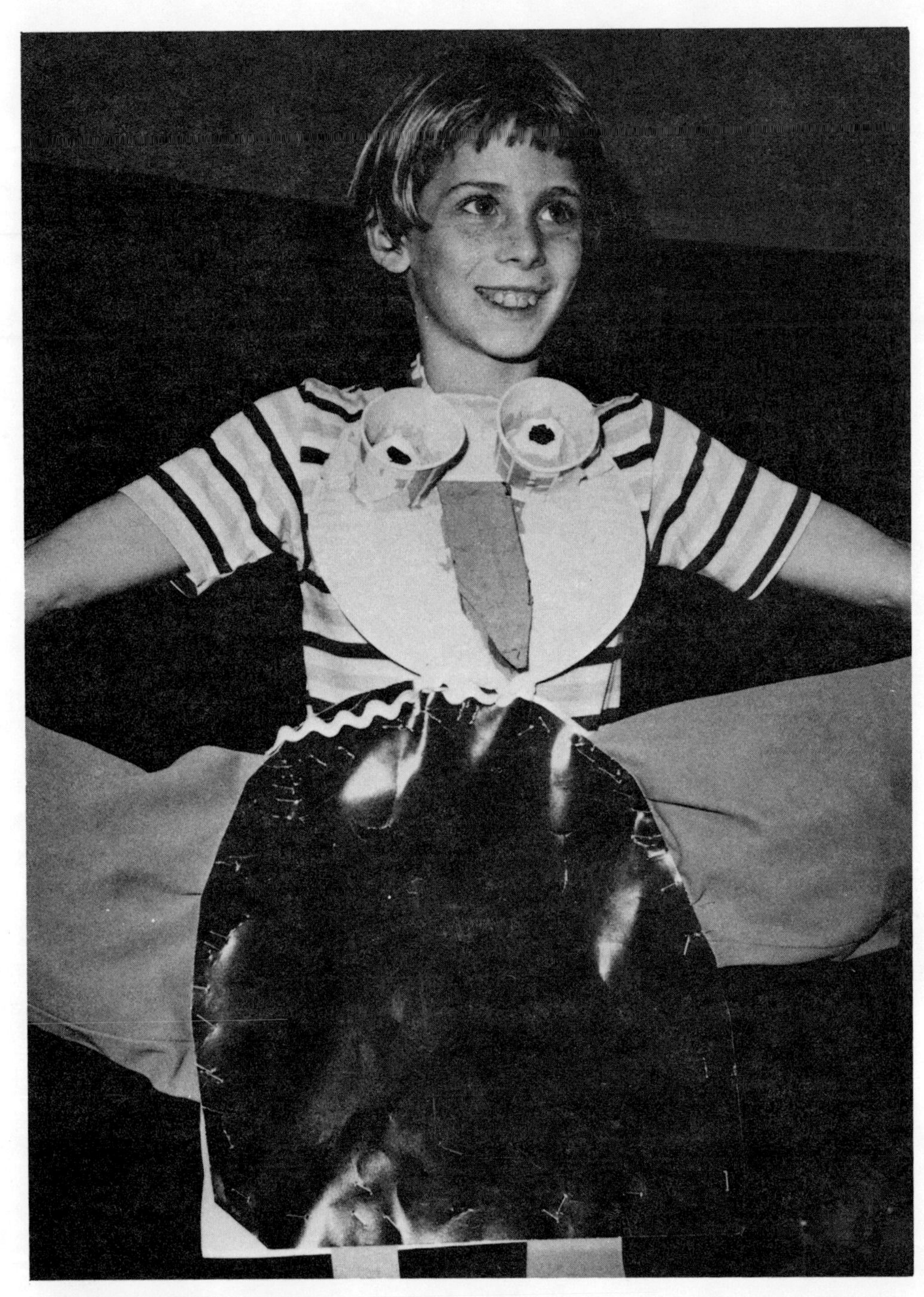

BODY PUPPET—Royal Bass
Owl

SOURCES OF MATERIAL AND INFORMATION

BODY PUPPET—Tracy Jarman
Lion

Organizations

PUPPETEERS OF AMERICA—A national organization for the betterment of puppetry, with membership from many parts of the world. An excellent source of inspiration and cohesiveness, it offers: an annual Puppet Festival, held in various parts of the country; the Puppetry Store for purchasing books and puppet items, a bi-monthly magazine; consultant services in all areas of puppetry; and affiliated guilds located in various regions of the country. A small membership fee is required. For information, write to: Puppeteers of America, Gayle G. Schluter, Treasurer, #5 Cricklewood Path, Pasadena, CA 91107.

PUPPETRY IN EDUCATION—A new organization that formed in 1977 because of the growing interest of puppetry in education. Its purpose is to serve as a resource center and puppet store and help unite and share ideas among educators in all areas of puppetry through a monthly newsletter. A small membership fee is required. Write to: Puppetry In Education Project, 164 27th Street, San Francisco CA 94110.

NATIONAL STORYTELLING RESOURCE CENTER—An organization specializing in exploring and upgrading the quality of storytelling techniques. It holds an annual storytelling convention as well as serves as a comprehensive resource center. A special grant is making it possible for this group to compile a unique collection of folk tales. Write to National Storytelling Resource Center, P.O. Box 112, Jonesborough TN 37659.

ONTARIO PUPPETRY ASSOCIATION—A Canadian puppetry organization offering various activities and services. Write to: Kenneth McKay, Executive Secretary, 10 Skyview Crescent, Willowdale, Ontario M2J 1B8, Canada.

BRITISH PUPPET CENTRE—A British group offering various services. Write to: British Puppet Centre, Battersea Town Hall, Lavender Hill, London S.W.11, England.

BRITISH PUPPET AND MODEL THEATRE GUILD—A British group offering various services. Write to: British Puppet and Model Theatre Guild, Mr. G. Shapley, Hon. Secretary, 7 Lupus Street, London SW, England.

THE EDUCATIONAL PUPPETRY ASSOCIATION—A British group involved in using puppetry in education. Write to: Mr. A. R. Philpott, Director, 23A Southampton Place, London WC1A, 2BP, England.

UNIMA ORGANIZATIONS—An international organization with a broad range of activities, including an international annual festival, held at various parts of the world. Write to: *in USA* UNIMA, Mrs. Mollie Falkenstein, General Section of UNIMA, 132 Chiquita Street, Laguna Beach CA 92651; or Mr. Jan Bussell, 16 Riverside, Egham, Surrey, England.

Puppet Manufacturers

NANCY RENFRO STUDIOS—Offers a unique, inexpensive line of over 300 whimsical puppet characters, specifically designed for loan services, storytelling and show productions within the library system. Puppets for circulation are rugged and washable mitt-type puppets that can easily be packaged in loan bags. Librarians can interchange puppets periodically with books, filmstrips, cassettes and other media. Included in the selection are: almost every type of animal imaginable (anteater, penguin, platypus, octopus, minnow, crab, shrew, raccoon, shark, donkey, are a few examples); representational puppets (such as rain, night and day, house, flower, etc); people (of any flesh tone or nationality); and fairy tale characters. The company also carries a line of educational puppets, show puppets, scripts and cassette puppet plays. Write to: Nancy Renfro Studios, 1117 W. 9th Street, Austin TX 78703.

POSSUM TROT—Markets an extensive line of cuddly, furry animal characters. Includes woodland creatures such as bunnies and opossums as well as a variety of other animals. Very appealing. Write to: Possum Trot, P.O. Box 249, McKee KY 40447.

MARY MEYERS—Puts out a line of appealing hand puppets in various people characters, with funny noses and personalities. Write to: Mary Meyer Mfg., Townshend VT 05353.

POPPETS—Has available a line of animal characters in a Muppet-like style. Write to: Poppetts, 1800 E. Olive Way, Seattle WA 98102.

ANNIE DEMPSEY—Creates a line of imaginatively crocheted puppets of a more expensive nature, bordering on fantasy. Write to: Annie Dempsey, 4829 Viewmon Street, Holladay UT 94117.

PUPPET FRIENDS—Constructs nicely made, soft and appealing animal and people puppets. Write to: Puppet Friends, 24022 A. Vista Montana, Torrance CA 90505.

PUPPETRY IN EDUCATION—Serves as a resource center for puppetry items and has available puppets, books, and kits. Write to: PIE, 164 27th Street, San Francisco CA 94110.

PUPPET FACTORY—Markets a line of inexpensive, lovable puppet characters, including a knobby-kneed bird, hippy, turtle and other imaginative creatures. Write to Puppet Factory, 160 S. Whisman Road, Mountain View CA 94041.

REEVES INTERNATIONAL, INC.—Distributes high-quality, more expensive line of German made "Steiff" and "Kersa" brand puppets. Write to: Reeves International, Inc., 1107 Broadway, New York NY 10010.

IRENE HEILAND—Created the playful puppets for the James A. Mitehener Library as shown in this book on page 81. She custom makes similar puppets for libraries. Write to: Irene Heiland, Route No. 1, Box 133, Coopersburg PA 18036.

HAPPY HOLLOW PUPPETS, INC.—Creates custom made puppets and scenery to order. Write to: Happy Hollow Puppets, Inc., 324 Zorn Avenue, Louisville KY 40206.

L. K. HECHT CO., INC.—Carries a line of nicely detailed finger puppets. Write to: L. K. Hecht Company, Inc., 1140 Broadway, New York NY 10001.

LESWING PRESS—Sells fairy tale sets in both hand and finger puppets, which include scripts and instructions for play production. Larger puppets are in a Muppet style. Write to: Leswing Press, 750 Adrian Way, San Rafael CA 94903.

PUPPET PRODUCTIONS—Carries an extensive line of colorful, muppet-like people of varied flesh tones. Also a line of funloving animal puppets. This company markets an extensive selection of scripts and cassette tapes geared to Bible and Sunday school themes. Write to: Puppet Productions, P.O. Box 82008, San Diego CA 92138.

DOUGLASS COMPANY, INC.—Markets puppets with "Cat in the Hat" and "Sam I Am" highlights. Write to: Douglass Company, Inc., Keene NH.

PACK-A-LUCK—Markets a line of cute animal and people hand puppets which feature a flexible "sock" talking mouth. Write to: Pack-a-Luck, P.O. Box 18610, Tucson AZ.

R. DAKIN & COMPANY—This toy manufacturer has a large selection of puppets in various types and materials. Write to: R. Dakin, P.O. Box 7746, Rincon Anex, San Francisco CA 94120.

FAO SCHWARZ—This well-known toy store offers a constant collection of quality puppets from around the world. Write to: FAO Schwarz, Fifth and 58th Street, New York NY 10022.

For more addresses and information on puppet manufacturers and sources, write to: TOY MANUFACTURERS OF AMERICA, 200 Fifth Avenue, New York NY 10010.

Stages and Equipment

PUPPET HARDWARE and MURRY'S HELLO PUPPETS—Offer excellent stages to libraries and professionals. Both feature portable and collapsible types as well as custom to individual needs. The former constructs with steel piping, the latter with wood framing. Write to: Puppet Hardware, 739 Ecton Road, Akron OH 44304 or Murry's Hello Puppets, 317 Alverno Road, Media PA 19063.

GAYLORD BROS., INC.—Markets a lightweight, plastic corrugated small stage with window opening, ideal for a puppet corner or informal table-top performances, seen on page 51. Order #L 104, Cost: $23.00. Write to: Gaylord Bros., Inc., Box 61, Syracuse NY 13201.

Recording

THE KING STREET RECORDING COMPANY—Offers custom recording, editing and duplication of tapes, cassettes, and 8-track cartridges. Poor recordings can be improved, and damaged recordings repaired. Complete sound tracks with voices, music and sound effects can be created for plays, puppet shows and audio-visual presentations. Write or call: The King Street Recording Company, P.O. Box 402, Malvern PA 19355 (215) 647-4341.

Puppet Supplies

MANGELSEN'S—This craft supply shop carries an excellent supply of doll heads, eyes and other accessories, useful for making puppets. They also have some puppet making books and patterns. Write to: Mangelsen's, 3457 South 84th Street, Omaha NE 68124.

CENTRAL SHIPPE—Markets a line of inexpensive felt puppet kits. Write to: Central Shippe/Allied Felt Corporation, 44 Starlake, Bloomingdale NJ

FREEMOUNTAIN TOYS, INC.—Order from this company for Vogue "Vegimal." Collection of funny and colorful food-shaped dolls, with a few surprises, such as peas with faces (inside a zip-up pod, etc.), convert into puppets. Write to: Freemountain Toys, Inc., Bristol VT 05443.

EASTERN MILLS—Supplies felt of wide color selection. Write to: Eastern Mills, Box 154, Chelsea MA 02150.

AMERICAN HANDICRAFTS CO.—Supplies craft items such as styrofoam balls and eyes. Write to: American Handicrafts Co., P.O. Box 1643, Fort Worth TX.

Puppet Books

Paperback Educational Series. Order from: Nancy Renfro Studios, 1117 W. 9th Street, Austin, Tx 78703.

A PUPPET CORNER IN EVERY LIBRARY, Nancy Renfro—A practical handguide for the librarian, on puppetry application to library purposes. $8.95. 1978, Nancy Renfro Studios.

PUPPETRY AND CREATIVE DRAMATICS IN STORYTELLING, Connie Champlin; illustrated by Nancy Renfro—A superb book for adapting traditional and modern stories with puppets and creative dramatics activities. Easy-to-follow projects for group storytelling with preschool through grade 6. $9.95. 1980 Nancy Renfro Studios.

PUPPETRY AND THE ART OF STORY CREATION, Nancy Renfro—An inspiring book on creative story development for puppet plays. Includes many ideas for language arts, the special child, puppet-making and exploring the imagination. Grade 1 through 6. $10.95. 1979 Nancy Renfro Studios.

MAKE AMAZING PUPPETS, Beverly Armstrong and Nancy Renfro—A jammed-packed booklet of easy and clever puppet-making ideas from recycled materials. Handy for any youth group instructor. $3.95. 1980 Learning Works.

The following puppetry books and items are taken from an annotated list (condensed), compiled by the Puppetry Store. All items are available from:

THE PUPPETEERS OF AMERICA'S PUPPETRY STORE

14316 Sturtevant Road
Silver Spring, Md. 20904

BOOKS

THE ART OF THE PUPPET, Bil Baird—Puppets throughout the ages, covering all forms and types from all sections of the globe are presented. $19.95. 1966, Plays.

THE COMPLETE BOOK OF PUPPETRY, David Currell—A book of value for all puppeteers, from beginner to advanced. Methods of constructing and manipulating puppets of all kinds are given in detail, accompanied by clear, easy-to-follow diagrams. $14.95. 1975, Plays.

DICTIONARY OF PUPPETRY, A. R. Philpott—Technical, historical and biographical aspects of puppetry covered in this comprehensive handbook. $8.95. 1969, Plays.

THE DWIGGINS MARIONETTES, Dorothy Abbe—A complete experimental theatre in miniature. A comprehensive record of one man's experiments with the puppet theatre. $29.95. 1970, Plays.

EASY TO MAKE PUPPETS, Joyce Luckin—Over 20 puppets, mostly made of felt, are described, including both hand puppets and marionettes, $4.95. 1975, Plays.

EIGHT PLAYS FOR HAND PUPPETS, Educational Theatre Association—These plays have proved successful and are particularly suitable for school use. Many animal characters are used and the scenery is simple. $4.00. 1968, Plays.

EXPERT PUPPET TECHNIQUE, Eric Bramall and Christopher Somerville—A manual of production for puppeteers by two master puppet showmen. Discuss scenic and puppet design, lighting, sound, movement, and manipulation, and offer suggestions on writing plays and conducting rehearsals. $4.95. 1966, Plays.

FELT TOY MAKING: ADVANCED TECHNIQUES, Amy. Van Gilder—Nine unusual felt puppets make up the first half of the book. Toys in the last half of the books could be made into puppets with few changes. $9.95. 1974, Drake Publication.

FOLK PUPPET PLAYS FOR THE SOCIAL STUDIES, Margaret Weeks Adair and Elizabeth Patapoff—Sixteen puppet plays suitable for schoolroom production have been adapted from American and other ethnic tales; presented in quick and simple techniques. $9.95. 1972, John Day.

HAND PUPPETS: HOW TO MAKE AND USE THEM, Laura Ross—The emphasis is on paper bag puppets, papier maché puppets, and shadow puppets. Three plays are included—Rumpelstiltskin, Punch & Judy, and an original play by the author, A Visit to Outer Space. $5.95 hardback, $2.95 paperback. 1969, Lothrop.

HOW TO BE A PUPPETEER, Eleanor Boylan—"What to do" with a puppet once it's made. Discusses building a script from a simple story, and stresses effective production. Six plays for home or classroom. $4.95. 1970, Dutton.

LET'S START A PUPPET THEATRE, Benny E. Andersen—Concerns making hand puppets and rod puppets. Many suggestions for simple stages, lighting and sound. $4.95. 1973, Van Nos Reinhold.

MAKING & USING FINGER PUPPETS, Margaret Hutchings—Finger puppets for sewers, knitters, and "stickers" (or pasters). Includes patterns for animals, a clown, and an entire Punch and Judy show. $8.50. 1973, Taplinger.

MAKING GLOVE PUPPETS, Esmé McLarne—This volume is noteworthy for the many full size animal patterns from which tracings can be made directly. $12.95. 1973, Plays.

MAKING PUPPETS COME ALIVE, Larry Engler and Carol Fijan—A method of teaching hand puppetry, which has been called "The Stanislavsky of the puppet world." Good puppet theatrical technique, including voice use, improvisation, role characterization and other fundamental elements are covered in relaxed, readable style. $9.95. 1973, Taplinger.

MARIONETTES: HOW TO MAKE AND WORK THEM, Helen Filing—A complete book of marionette craft, including the producing of shows, for the beginning puppeteer. $2.75. 1973, Dover.

PENNY PUPPETS, PENNY THEATRE AND PENNY PLAYS, Moritz Jagendorf—Explicit directions for making inexpensive puppets with diagrams of necessary scenery and costumes. Written simply so it may be used by children 8-10 years of age. Includes nine puppet plays. $69.95. 1941, Plays.

PLAYING WITH PUPPETS, Lis Paludan—An excellent book for the young or beginning puppeteer, with many patterns. Primarily on the making and manipulation of hand puppets, it also includes material on rod puppets, stages, scenery, etc., as well as seven short plays and play ideas. $7.95. 1975, Plays.

PUNCH AND JUDY, Ed Emberley—A Punch and Judy to be enjoyed for its delightful illustrations which fill every page. $4.95. 1965, Little.

THE PUPPET BOOK, Wall, White and Philpott—Discusses all forms of puppetry, all types of construction with clear diagrams, plus chapters on plays and production. A couple of short hand puppet plays are included. $8.95. 1950, Plays.

PUPPET CIRCUS, Peter Praser—Instructions for the traditional circus puppets, plus old toy puppets. All aspects of their construction fully described with complete diagrams and instructions for production. $5.95.

A PUPPET CORNER IN EVERY LIBRARY, Nancy Renfro—A practical handguide for the librarian, on puppetry application to library purposes. $7.95. 1978, Nancy Renfro Studios.

PUPPET MAKING THROUGH THE GRADES, Grisella Hopper—A book for young people, for teachers, and for others who work with children. Paper bags, boxes, socks, balloons, styrofoam and many other everyday items combine to form appealing puppets. $6.50. Davis.

PUPPET PLAYS FOR YOUNG PLAYERS, Lewis Mahlmann & David C. Jones—Twelve fast-paced scripts include original plays, adaptations, dramatizations, even spoofs on familiar fairy tales, legends and classics. $7.95. 1974, Plays.

PUPPET THEATRE HANDBOOK, Marjorie Batchelder—The Handbook covers practically every phase of puppet construction and production, bringing together contributions of technical knowledge from more than 50 outstanding puppeteers. Includes bibliography and materials. $9.95. 1947, Harper & Row.

THE PUPPET THEATRE IN AMERICA, Paul McPharlin; supplement by Marjorie McPharlin—An authentic and complete history of the growth of the puppet art in America. Many rare and unusual prints in the original text. $12.95. 1969, Plays.

THE PUPPET THEATRE OF JAPAN, A. C. Scott—It traces the history of Bunraku from its earliest days to the present and explains the role of the puppeteer, the narrator and the musician in this technique of puppetry. $3.50 paperbound. 1973, C.E. Tuttle.

THE PUPPET THEATRE OF THE MODERN WORLD, Compiled by UNIMA Editorial Board, Margareta Niculescu, Chairman—A handsome volume similar to the Baird book but less history and more stress on the art of the puppet theatre. $14.95. 1967, Plays.

THE PUPPETEER'S LIBRARY GUIDE, Vol. 1: The Historical Background Puppetry and its Related Fields, J. Francis Crothers—Included in the vast amount of material are bibliographies of puppet literature, and material on organizations and publications devoted to puppetry. $17.00. 1971, Scarcrow.

PUPPETS, Barbara Snook—Clear drawings and precise instructions give information on hand puppets, their costumes and stages. Marionettes are dealt with in even greate rdetail. $4.75. 1966, Branford.

PUPPETS FOR BEGINNERS, Moritz Jagendorf—Imaginative and colorful pictures help beginners create and use hand puppets and marionettes, make the stage and costumes. Recommended for ages 7-12. $4.95. 1952, Plays.

PUPPETS FOR PLAY PRODUCTION, Nancy Renfro—Puppets of every description made from odds and ends of every description. Good for the pre-school child or for the teacher. Combines creative thinking with definite plans of procedure. Out of print. $6.95. 1969, Crowell.

PUPPETS THAT ARE DIFFERENT, Audrey Vinvente Dean—A dragon, a snake charmer and snake, a lion, and a horse are just some of the hand puppets that can be made from patterns and diagrams in this book. $7.95. 1974, Taplinger.

SHADOW PUPPETS IN COLOR, Louise Cochrane—This is for the beginner in shadow puppetry, or the young puppeteer. Three shadow plays are included, one from each country where this type of puppetry flourished: A Chinese legend, a play from the Greek shadow theater, and a Hindu-Japanese legend.

$4.95. 1972, Plays.

SHADOW PUPPETS, SHADOW THEATRES AND SHADOW FILMS, Lotte Reiniger *new edition*—The most complete book on shadow puppetry available by a world-famous expert. $10.00. 1975, Plays.

SKITS AND PUPPETS, O. W. Bennett—Actually a manual written for Boy Scouts by a Scout official. Fine for girls also, or anyone teaching puppetry to the 6-12 age group. $.65 paperbound. 1967, BSA.

TOM TICHENOR'S PUPPETS, Tom Tichenor—Gives directions for making and costuming both hand puppets and marionettes, for acquiring stage and props, for bringing the puppet to life. Includes three plays for hand puppets and four for marionettes. $6.95. 1971, Abingdon.

THE WONDERFUL WORLD OF PUPPETS, Günter Böhmer—A beautiful book written by the manager of the Puppet Collection of the City of Munich, Germany. Discusses the history of puppetry and illustrates it with 76 black and white and 16 pages of color from that collection. $8.95. 1971, Plays.

YOU CAN BE A PUPPETEER, Carolyn London—Describes various types of puppets and how to make them simply and inexpensively. Several plays are included, some of them based on favorite Bible characters. $2.50 paperbound. 1972, Moody.

PAMPHLETS

BLACK THEATRE, Coad Canada Puppets—This theatrical staging technique, relatively new to North America, is well explained and clearly diagrammed. $3.00.

BRING ON THE PUPPETS! Helen Ferguson—Simple puppets for use in church-school teachings are described and illustrated including patterns. For different age levels. Six plays using various kinds of puppets, among them "The Christmas story" and "The Story of Hanukkah." $3.25.

CLASSROOM STAGES, Coad Canada Puppets—It contains detailed plans and explanation of five different kinds of stages, plus a "versatile" stage which can be converted to many uses. $3.00.

FELT PUPPETS, Harold Mangelsen and Sons—Contains detailed instruction and patterns for seventeen hand puppets made of felt. $1.25.

A MANUAL OF HAND PUPPET MANIPULATION, Lettie Connell Schubert—So little has been written on this subject that not only beginners in hand puppetry but even "experienced" puppeteers would benefit from the experiments and exercises suggested. $1.25.

PUPPENSPIEL IN GRAPHIC UND MALEREI: ITALIEN, Hans R. Purschke—This is the first publication devoted entirely to puppet graphics. This first collection shows Italian puppetry through 53 pictures. $2.75.

PUPPENSPIEL IN GRAPHIC UND MALEREI: DEUTSCHLAND I—This collection has just been published, and will be followed by collections of etchings, lithographs and paintings from France, England, etc. $2.75.

PUPPET THEATRE MANAGEMENT, Coad Canada Puppets—Outlines step by step the business operation involved in a successful puppet theater. Invaluable help for the beginning puppeteer. Bibliography. $3.00.

PUPPETRY IN RELIGIOUS EDUCATION, Rev. William Jacoby—A mimeographed booklet by a minister who used puppets frequently in his church services. $1.25.

PUPPETS FOR THE CLASSROOM, Alison Vandergun—A book for teachers who wish to introduce puppetry into the classroom. Puppets are designed to be quick and simple to make, and easy to teach. A loose folded sheet of patterns is included. $2.50.

PUPPETS FROM POLYFOAM: SPONGE-EES, Bruce Chessé and Beverly Armstrong—There is special emphasis on construction of features in this book of guidelines for using polyfoam to construct quick and interesting hand puppets with glue or staple gun. $2.50. 1975, Early Stages.

PUPPETS OF AUSTRALIA, Compiled by Norman Hetherington—The work of 38 puppeteers or puppet companies is presented in this pamphlet made possible by the Australian Council for the Arts. $2.50.

ROD PUPPETS, Coad Canada Puppets—Clear and precise diagrams and illustrations with tips on fabrics, paints, and other materials to make rod puppets. $2.00.

SHADOW PUPPET KNOW-HOW, Betty Polus—A pamphlet packed with information of the fundamentals of shadow puppet materials and techniques. $2.00.

START WITH A BALLOON, R. C. Nick LeFeuvre—A step-by-step explanation of the method used in making puppet hands using a balloon as a base. $.65.

USING PUPPETS IN SCHOOLS, Coad Canada Puppets—The emphasis in this publication is on the effective use of hand puppets in a school situation rather than on puppet construction. $3.00.

INDIVIDUAL PLAYS

THE SILVER SERIES OF PUPPET PLAYS—Nineteen plays, many adapted from the classics, others written especially for this series. $1.00 each. Branden Publications: *Horns Of The Moon,* Lisl Beer; *Somebody—Nothing* (Ancient Japanese Farce), edited by Lisl Beer; *The Unwilling Doctor,* Moliere; *Kasper, The Portrait Painter,* Franz Pocci; *Punch and Judy,* from several texts, edited by Lisl Beer; *Sir Eglamore and the Dragon,* Lisl Beer; *Jonah and the Whale,* Lisl Beer; *Only Three Wishes,* Challis Walker; *Orlando Furioso,* Adrian Van de Horst; *The Two Deaf Men,* Victor E. Francois; *The Wishing Fairy,* Franz Pocci; *Great Is Kush,* Lisl Beer; *Second Shepherd's Play,* from the Townley Cycle Manuscript; *The Prince and the Mermaid,* Lisl Beer; *The Emperor and the Nightinggale,* Hans Christian Andersen; *Mr. Vinegar,* Lisle Beer; *The Neighbors,* Louis-Emile Duranty; *Chimpanzee, The Darwin Ape,* Franz Pocci; *Punch Plays Teacher,* Louis-Emile Duranty.

1970 AWARD WINNING PLAYS

BAD LUCK, GOOD LUCK, Wanda Korybut—Peter, a poor peasant lad who attributed his wealthy cousin's success to good luck, goes in search of a mythical character, his own Good Luck. He is thwarted by a haunted house, skeletons and a dragon. Written for hand puppets. Playing time one hour. $1.25.

SPACESHIP TO CLOUDLAND, Harold Lynch—Benjy and Professor Von Bump have a thrilling adventure in a space ship, which, out of control, visits Cloudland, Balloonville and Cloud Mouse Country. Written for marionettes including a "break-away" giant. About one hour playing time. $1.25.

THE OCCUPANTS, Eleanor Boyland—That wonderful night in Bethlehem, as told by the animals in the stable. Original music included. About 50 minutes playing time. $1.25.

ADDITIONAL PLAYS

PLAYS ADAPTED BY HELEN HAIMAN JOSEPH—Ali Baba; Cinderella; Hansel and Gretel; Jack and the Beanstalk; Pinocchio; Sleeping Beauty; Snow White. $1.00 each.

THE SACRED HORSE, Vivian Michael—A puppet play for rod puppets or marionettes. Not for beginners. Friendship is the theme of this play which can become a dramatic performance with all the atmosphere of old China. $1.25.

THE THREE WISHES. Vivian Michael—An interesting version of this age-old tale of the woodcutter and the "sausages." For hand puppets or marionettes. $1.25.

TWO CHRISTMAS PUPPET PLAYS—Two plays, *Little Lost Angel* by Sarah Leslie, and *The Christmas Stowaway* by Hazel Royce Gowdy. Reprinted from the Puppetry Journal. $1.00

MISCELLANEOUS

CLOTH HAND PUPPET PATTERN, Lewis Mahlmann—For those who like to sew—not the rag doll type but a shaped puppet pattern that even permits you to change the profile of the face for various characters. Step by step, very definite instructions. $1.25.

All plays royalty free to members of Puppeteers of America

Additional Publications

PUPPETS FOR DREAMING AND SCHEMING, Judy Sims and Beverly Armstrong—A new sourcebook for those doing educational puppetry with children. Packed with imaginative ideas, scripts, lessons and patterns. Write to: Early Stages, P. O. Box 5027, Walnut Creek CA 94596.

BOOKLETS ABOUT PUPPETS, Betty Polus—A varied selection of themes is offered here, such as: bread-dough puppets; doorway puppet stages; a bilingual puppetry experience; shadow puppets; and lighting a stage. Betty Polus suggested the ideas for "Mice are Nice" elsewhere in this book. Write to: Betty Polus Folk Puppet Theater, 14755 Two Bar Road, Boulder Creeks CA 95006.

PUPPET PLAYS FROM FAVORITE STORIES, Lewis Hahlmann and David Cadwalader Jones—A new collection of one-act plays adapted from famous fairy tales and stories. Plays, Inc.

LEARNING THROUGH PUPPETS, Annie Aleskovsky—A good book with a simple approach to using puppets in plays. Scripts include special learning experiences for children, covering themes such as "teasing" and "being small." Allen Raymond, Inc. Publishing.

PACK-O-FUN—Is a monthly craft magazine that incorporates puppet patterns and ideas from time to time. Write to: Pack-O-Fun, 14 Main Street, Park Ridge IL 60068.

PUPPETRY, THE ULTIMATE DISGUISE, George Latshaw—An excellent theater handbook written by a master to train the student in areas of design, construction, production and other facets of puppeteering. Richard Rosen Press, Inc.

PUPPETS AND THERAPY, A. R. Philpott—This book brings together innovative ideas and experiments in the use of puppets and puppetry with the handicapped, the emotionally and mentally impaired. Plays, Inc.

THE ART OF MAKING PUPPETS AND MARIONETTES, Charleen Davis Roth—A good book for making soft puppets of varied types, including patterns for lovable animals. Chilton Book Company.

LET'S START A PUPPET THEATRE, Benny E. Andersen—An excellent book on fresh ideas in puppet making of all sorts, stages and general advice. Van Nos Reinhold. The Know How Book of Puppets, Violet Philpott and Mary Jean McNeil. Simple ideas on imaginative puppet making. Sterling Publishing Company.

Publishers of Plays and Materials for Children's Theatre

ANCHORAGE PRESS, INC., Cloverlot, Anchorage, Kentucky 40223

THE COACH HOUSE PRESS, INC., 53 West Jackson Blvd., Chicago IL 60604

NEW PLAYS FOR CHILDREN, Box 273, Rowayton, Ct. 10685

YOUNG AUDIENCE SCRIPTS, 9140-146 A Street, Edmonton, Alberta, Canada

NEW PLAYS CATALOGUE, c/o Beverly Sturgill, 576 Polk Street, Twin Falls ID 83301

SAMUEL FRENCH, INC., 25 West 45th Street, New York NY 10036

THE DRAMATIC PUBLISHING COMPANY, 86 E. Randolph St., Chicago IL 60601

DRAMATISTS PLAY SERVICE, INC., 440 Park Avenue, South, New York NY 10016

PLAYS, INC., Publishers, 8 Arlington Street, Boston MA 02116

BAKER PLAYS, 100 Summer Street, Boston MA 02110

DAVI DMcCAY COMPANY, INC., 750 Third Avenue, New York.NY 10017

STAGE MAGIC PLAYS, P.O. Box 246, Schulenburg TX 78956

PIONEER DRAMA SERVICE, 2171 S. Colorado Blvd., Denver, CO 80222

PICKWICK PRESS, Box 4847, Midland TX 79701

INVOLVEMENT DRAMATICS, Oklahoma City University, N.W., 23rd and Blackwelder, Oklahoma City OK 73106

TAMS-WITMARK MUSIC LIBRARY, INC., 757 Third Avenue, New York NY 10017

ROGERS AND HAMMERSTEIN LIBRARY, 538 Madison Avenue, New York NY 10022

MUSIC THEATRE INTERNATIONAL, 119 West 57th St., New York NY 10019

THEATRE ARTS BOOKS, 333 Sixth Avenue, New York NY 10014

Films

ABC OF PUPPETMAKING (10 minutes) Part one and part two available. Bailey Films, Inc., 6509 De Longe Avenue, Hollywood CA.

LET'S MAKE PUPPETS (11 minutes) Visual Aids Service, University of Illinois, Division of Universtiy Extension, 704 S. Sixth Street, Champaign IL 61822

SIMPLE HAND PUPPETS (18 minutes) A Trend Production, by Walt Disney, 477 Madison Avenue, New York NY

Filmstrips

OLIVER, WILLIE AND PETER (a film strip about making puppets) The Dow Chemical Company, Distributed by Chartmakers, Inc., 480 Lexington Avenue, New York 17 NY

PUPPETS (35 minutes) Konrad Prothman, 2787 Milburn Avenue, Baldwin, L.I., NY